Observation

OBSERVATION

A flyfisher's guide to reading the water

Philip White

COCH-Y-BONDDU BOOKS
2016

OBSERVATION
A flyfisher's guide to reading the water
by Philip White

First published by Coch-y-Bonddu Books, Machynlleth, 2016

ISBN 978 1 904784 72 2

Coch-y-Bonddu Books Ltd
Machynlleth, Powys SY20 8DG
01654 702837
www.anglebooks.com

Printed and bound by Gomer Press, Wales, UK

Contents

List of Fly Dressings

List of Fly Dressings (continued)

Acknowledgements

This book would not have come about if it were not for two people in particular.

First, my wife Mary who has supported me through my years as a river keeper, often putting up with coming second to poacher patrols, hatchery work and my duties when working for the Duke of Rutland. She has also shared my more recent love affair with Lough Corrib and its near neighbours in Ireland where we now live, fish and walk together.

Second, John Wilshaw, who told me I could write, something my English masters at Grammar School would have challenged I am sure. He encouraged me back in the 1990's and I have written quite a lot over the years since then, mainly thanks to his influence.

Beyond that there are all those, too numerous to name, that I have met, fished with, and tied flies with. A few are named in the book while most are not but all have influenced my thinking and fly dressing over the years. Indeed, many are doing so still, be they beginners or world-renowned experts.

Now that I have decided to stop tweaking the content Paul Morgan has stepped up to the mark and said he will publish it so a big thank you to him as well.

Finally, a mention for the designer Pete MacKenzie who has taken my amateur efforts and turned them into something to be proud of.

PHOTOGRAPHS

The pictures in the book are all my own work, with the exception of those that feature me or my hands. These are all Mary's work, often taken in tricky conditions. Neither of us are photographers of any great experience so you have them 'warts and all.'

Introduction

During my life working in fishing I have known anglers of all abilities and from all walks of life. I have met anglers who only use one fly right through the season and I have also met anglers with so many flies that they could neither recognize nor know what to fish where or when. Both types of angler catch fish but their success can be limited on days when the fish are feeding very selectively. On these days you are not going to catch at all unless you have the right range of flies in your box. If you only fish one fly or you don't understand the contents of your fly box then you are not going to be properly armed so in this little book I am going to explain the simple relationships between fly life-cycles and trout behaviour as well as explain the wider 'larder' of trout food in a simple and easy to understand way. Most books on angling entomology take a scientific stance which I wish to avoid, preferring to keep it uncomplicated, so I am offering a simple insight into the fly hatches, other important insects and larger life-forms that all make up the diet of the trout and the other freshwater fish we target with a fly rod. I am also going to give pointers on how to recognise fish-holding water, both on rivers and lakes.

To me the ability to read the water is the most important element in fishing for all species of fish. It is more important than the ability to cast further than everyone around you. It is more important than having all the latest gear, expensive rods or fancy waistcoats, and it is more important than paying to fish the most expensive waters. To quote Ray Mears, survival expert and outdoorsman, 'Knowledge is far more important than equipment.' If you always fish with a guide then you are paying him to read the water for you, which is fine first time out on a new water, but if you want to get the best out of your fishing, you must learn to read the water for yourself. I have spent over 40 years working in flyfishing in one way or another, with most of that time spent as either river keeper or fishing guide/casting instructor and I have taught fly dressing

A plump wild Corrib trout in the net.

for even longer. As a guide I always try to explain the reasoning behind the decisions I make on the day, particularly to the more experienced rods and, where possible, I walk the river with them, pointing out what I expect to see happen during the day. I do the same in a boat, explaining why I am setting the boat the way I have, where I expect to find the fish and what to look out for. It was on such a river guiding day that one of my clients said that I should put down in a book all that we had talked about as most of it he had never even thought about before, despite being an experienced angler. This book is the result.

For me, the road to successful flyfishing is well signposted if you care to take a look and reading the water is no more difficult than reading a map. By reading the signs properly – and they are always there – you can find the right destination, a fish in the net. There are two main types of sign to look out for, as there are when driving.

First, there are the direction signs, which tell you about the water you are fishing, as covered in the chapter *Understanding your Water and its Topography*. These will point you to the feeding lies.

Second, there are the information signs which tell you about the fly hatches and other food items influencing the fishing, as covered

in the chapter on *Understanding the Larder*. Sometimes there are single signs, e.g. a mayfly or buzzer hatch with rising fish which makes finding the right road easy. At other times, there are many signs together, all apparently pointing to the same destination but via different roads, e.g. blue winged olive and pale watery spinners falling, blue winged olive duns and various caddis all hatching all at the same time just before darkness falls. Similar situations occur on lakes with mixed hatches of fly and falls of terrestrials as well as spinners and other egg-layers all happening at the same time. This more complex scenario makes finding your destination, that fish in the net, harder but by no means impossible. You may well have to try more roads until you find the right one but, if you understand the larder, your choice will be easier. The signs are all there, you just have to read them correctly.

Going back a little wiser

As you embark on this road to more successful flyfishing take a good look at the first chapter, entitled *Understanding your Quarry*. Throughout history successful generals have worked on the principal of 'know your enemy' – and fishing is no different. If you know how a trout or other target fish functions you have a better chance of catching it. There is no point in marching upright along the edge of the bank if the fish can see you or hear you and/

Smothered in early morning caenis. They got everywhere. Eyes, ears, specs lenses. Talk about a blizzard!

or feel your vibrations and there is little point in casting a dry-fly to a fish that is feeding three feet down on shrimps. So, plan your route carefully from the time you acquire your flies to the moment you lift your rod to make the first cast, whether you are fishing for trout in a chalkstream or bonefish on a tropical flat. The only thing that is different is the larder in your fly box.

Part One

READING THE WATER

A wild Lathkill brown trout at rest showing the red flanks and orange fins for which these fish are renowned. Above the red lateral line spots the olive brown back is peppered with small black spots.

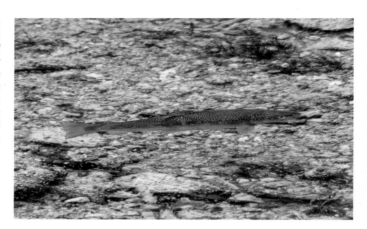

A Mask fish taken from open water. This fish has a deeply forked tail and is showing only black spots and a fairly silver colouration

Also a Mask fish but this time from a secluded bay close to the bank. Both older and larger this fish is brightly coloured with numerous red spots, russet flanks and a spade-like tail.

Understanding your Quarry

In order to be successful at catching your trout, or any other fish for that matter, you need to understand a little about it. We do not need a biology lesson here so let's keep it simple. Mother Nature designed fish to live and feed in water and gave them well developed senses to enable them to do so.

SHAPE AND COLORATION

Trout, as with all fish, are designed to suit their environment. They have a streamlined body with a mucus coating that allows them to slip easily through even the fastest water. Their internal swim-bladder and fins give them balance and ease of movement as well as helping them with stability and steering. Spend just a few moments watching a trout in a river and you will see just how effortlessly they can sit in a fast current with little need for tail power and how they move to and fro, intercepting tasty morsels of food with only the slightest movement of the pectoral fins or a slight twist of the tail. While they are true masters of the currents, they are equally at home in lakes. Here they swim around effortlessly when feeding, turning this way and that to intercept their food rising through the water column or being carried by the surface drift created by the wind. When feeding on fry their muscular body allows them to explode into action, charging into the shoals to stun the small fish with the bulk of their bodies prior to cruising round to pick off the dead and the dying one by one. When they are not feeding, the fish simply rest quietly waiting for the next feeding opportunity to arise.

We must not forget that trout are prey as well as predator so, as well as their natural speed and agility; they are well camouflaged by a combination of their spots and coloration, both of which vary according to the environment in which they live. In some waters the spot patterns are wide spread with large black spots over the backs and red 'port-hole' spots with gold rims along the flanks, while in other waters the black spots are much smaller and more closely patterned. In a peaty, moorland stream environment trout tend to be very dark brown on the back while chalkstream fish are more golden or even olive green. Some lake trout, like the Loch Leven strain, are less colourful, being silvery gold with black spots and few, if any red spots, while others, like the gillaroo strain from Ireland, are much more colourful, like their river brethren. Within this colour variation is the ability of the trout to change its colour somewhat to suit the river or lake bed it is on at any given moment. They can also vary this colour along the length of the body, appearing blotchy, thus breaking up their outline, something they will do when stressed. Many years ago I worked for a fishing club in East Sussex and their stock fish were delivered in silver-coloured tanks with mesh lids. The fish always arrived a drab blue/ grey colour with almost no hint of their usual brighter colours. They soon reverted once in the lakes but it was interesting to see.

SIGHT

Trout have good eyesight both in and out of water. Their eyes are on the sides of their head so some of their vision is binocular and some monocular. Feeding underwater is easy for them, particularly where they are using their binocular vision, whether seeking out shrimps and caddis on the gravel, taking nymphs off weed beds, intercepting ascending pupae, taking floating flies or chasing minnows. They are able to see behind at an upward angle but they are unable to see directly behind or below because of the position of their eyes.

The way they see out of the water through the surface is usually referred to as the 'cone of vision.' Biologists tell us there is an invisible, inverted cone shape up from the eyes, within which the light rays, or lines of sight, travel through the surface. These light rays are refracted at the surface such that the trout have a wider view out of the water than in it, being able to see to within around ten degrees of the surface. Anything in the air or on land below this line of sight is not readily visible to them. For this reason it is good to keep low when attempting to stalk fish as well as to keep the fly line low when casting. On the very edges of this cone of vision the trout's view is distorted, but remember, they are very tuned in to movement so care must still be exercised so as not to spook them, even when keeping low. Something as simple as a fly line flicking across their line of sight during casting is enough to put fish down. I have seen fish on the river Lathkill freeze and then slide slowly away after just one badly placed false cast, long before the fly was actually presented on the water.

Our biologists assure us that fish cannot see effectively out of the water outside this cone of vision. They tell us that light rays outside the cone are reflected back off the surface of the water and fish see only a reflection of their own environment here. For obvious reasons, this part of the surface is usually referred to as the

Rain on the lens as this Corrib five pounder is ready to go back. The fish's huge shoulders and deep body indicate the rich feeding in the lough. It picked out the footprint of my 'Hatching May' pattern in heavy rain.

mirror. However, this does not mean that a trout has no idea what is on the surface outside this cone of vision. I believe that what the fish sees is a distortion of this mirror, let's call it a 'footprint', created by the feet or body of the fly, beetle or what have you. This footprint is created by the dimples in the surface tension of the water where the feet and/or body of the insect touch the surface. In addition, many of the food items are moving, flapping wings or trying to walk on the surface. All of which send the right 'I am food' signals to the feeding fish below. I have seen it argued about winged dry flies that trout only rise to items on the surface once the wings come within their cone of vision. I do not agree. I am as certain as I can be that they respond to the footprint of floating food items and begin the rise process long before the fly is visible in the cone. N.B. Any food item that is actually trapped *in* the surface film is visible to the fish as at least part of the food item is below the surface. To a trout, recognising the footprint of a food item is no different from a countryman knowing at a glance the difference between a crow and a blackbird in flight. I have watched trout move yards sideways to intercept fully floating mayfly duns that were way outside any cone of vision, the fish clearly having seen the distortion of the surface film. The fish may still decide to abort the rise at the last moment, once he has a clearer view of the food item inside the cone of vision, but I believe he makes the first move early. The matter of wings I have just alluded to may well be a factor in the fish aborting at the last moment but I am sure they do not figure in the initial rise decision.

Trout respond very quickly to both movement and shadows because, as I have already said, while they are predators they are also prey and a lot of their predators are winged or land-based. The response of a trout to the flicker of shadow from a bird going across the line of the sun has to be seen to be believed so the need to keep the rod, fly line and yourself out of sight in every way is paramount. This includes flashy rod finishes (I have coated mine in matt varnish since the early 70's), inappropriate light-coloured clothing, bright fly lines and the like. I see a lot of anglers on green bushed English rivers wearing light tan or stone coloured clothing and casting high-visibility yellow fly lines. It would be much better to wear olive green and use dull, darker fly lines. I have long been an advocate for dark fly lines and, while I cannot prove anything scientifically, I have been videoed casting with light and dark lines together, and I am fully convinced. On numerous occasions I have watched fish freeze at the very first false cast before sliding quietly into hiding. In addition, fish will respond to changes in their horizons, as do deer and other prey animals, so, just because you are not moving, it does not mean that allowing your head and shoulders to poke above the fishes horizon is okay.

Trout see colour, including fluorescent colours, and I am convinced this is possible even at night, despite biologists saying otherwise. Why else do they hit a fly with a fluorescent hot spot in preference to one without, and how can they differentiate between an orange hackle and a light blue one at night unless they can see colour at night? I have had this happen on a number of occasions when fishing for sea-trout, tested by changing and re-changing flies when fish were hitting flies well.

HEARING

Trout have internal ears and have acute hearing for normal frequency sounds that are found in water. In addition, they have a very highly developed vibration-sensing system within the lateral line so they can 'hear' both normal and low frequency sounds well. This includes picking up on any form of vibration noise such as an angler walking along the bank, wading in the water or shuffling about in a boat, as well as bait-fish moving nearby. So when fishing, make your watchword *stealth*. Tread lightly and when you arrive at a run or pool, sit down and take your time before casting. In a boat, keep your feet as still as you can and avoid dropping things. However, it is unlikely they can hear you talking on the bankside as airborne sound does not transfer well into water as you will notice if you submerge in the swimming pool.

SENSE OF SMELL

Again, this is a very acute sense that allows the trout to find certain types of prey even in the dark, as well as finding their way about generally and warning them of the presence of foreign objects like men in waders upstream of them. New Zealand fishing guides have told me they can tell by the behaviour of the trout when other fishermen are wading a river, even a long way upstream, especially on the harder fished waters.

Remember, if you can see the trout then there is a very strong likelihood that he can see you and he probably heard or felt you arrive anyway. Adopt the advice of Izaak Walton, written in *The Compleat Angler* – "Study to be quiet."

A newly hatched mayfly dun sitting high on the film. The head-and-tail rise *is typical here.*

Dying spent mayfly spinner lying half drowned in the film. The sipping rise *is typical here.*

Feeding Depth and Rise Forms

Depth is a major factor in flyfishing, indeed all types of fishing, yet it is probably the least understood factor of all. That fish feed on a range of insects and other fauna is a given fact. This food may be on the surface, the bed of the lake or river or anywhere in between at any time of the day, depending upon prevailing conditions. It is up to us to find what it is the fish are feeding on as well as just how deep down the fish are feeding at any given time of day.

Observation of flies in the air, on the water or in the bushes will help to tell us what, whilst a combination of observation and experimentation will tell us the correct depth at any given point in time. The feeding depth is constantly varying according to the stage of the hatch, the time of day and weather conditions and the successful angler is the one who realises this and reacts accordingly.

WHERE ARE THE FISH FEEDING?

As with all good detective novels the solution is reached by following and interpreting the evidence. From the surface film right down to the bottom, fish can be feeding at any depth depending on the position of their food so, if the fish are not showing their feeding activity on the surface, it is up to you to find where they are in the water column. On clear rivers and lakes it is often possible to see the fish feeding at quite some depth. In this case it is much easier to adapt your tactics accordingly.

Just one word of warning here: the true depth is not always easy to assess in very clear rivers like the Lathkill in Derbyshire and the Lambourn in Berkshire, or on clear lakes like Lough Carra in Co. Mayo, Ireland, and getting the sub-surface fly down to fish feeding near the bottom takes more skill than some people realise. On waters where fish are not easily seen then tackling fishing at depth is really a matter of trial and error using a variety of differing fly weights and, especially on lakes, a variety of differing line densities until the feeding level is found.

ON FLIES AND LINES

To be properly equipped on a river you will need fly patterns that imitate adult flies and other egg-laying patterns to be fished on the surface, emergers to be fished half in and half out of the surface, lightweight sub-surface flies for the upper levels, medium weight mid-water flies and, finally, heavyweight deep-water flies plus a streamer or two, where allowed. I limit my own river trout fishing to floating lines these days unless I am fishing streamers that need to be on or near the bottom in deep water in which case sink tip or fully sinking lines are needed, depending on flow and depth.

On lakes of all sizes you may need all of these fly types as well as a wide range of sinking lines to get your flies where you need them. I have friends who fish competitions who have around twenty-four lines ready for immediate use every time they are out. I am not advocating this number for everyone as it is a pretty intense and specialised style of fishing, but a floater, sink tip, intermediate, clear intermediate and Type II, Type III and Type V sinkers are really a must for serious fishing on large English reservoirs and the deeper natural loughs and lochs of Ireland and Scotland. For me the floater and sink tip are the most favoured and the others are only very occasionally used. This is a matter of purely personal choice as far as I am concerned so my advice to all anglers is 'learn to master the depths as well as the tackle needed to fish them and your success rate will soar.'

DEPTH AND THE DRY-FLY

Even the simple concept of the surface fly has several facets to it. If fish are feeding at the surface making some form of surface-breaking rise pattern, what are they feeding on? Is it a newly hatched fly, emerger, terrestrial or egg-layer? Each of these has a specific position relative to the surface film. Starting at the top and working down we have the fully hatched flies standing on the surface making dimples in the film with their feet. These flies are usually easy to spot and easy to imitate with any one of thousands of modern and traditional dry flies. The rise form is usually a **head-and-tail rise** showing head, dorsal fin and tail in rotation. Down a step we have the surface egg-layers. These can be sitting quite high on the film in the early laying stages but the body will be touching the film as well, making a different footprint. Again a head and tail rise is the norm. For these flies we need to imitate them with artificials that sit lower on the surface, either by design or adaptation e.g., clipping the hackle flat underneath. Next we come to a more complex situation where we have fully spent spinners and sedges, as well as other egg-layers and terrestrials that sit fully in the film, semi-submerged. These are usually taken with a more **sipping rise** where just the tip of the nose breaks the surface. Close observation will often tell you what fly it is that is creating the rise and this is when the time spent looking in the vegetation as suggested in the previous chapter can start to pay off, having given you hints on what to look for. Finally we have the emerger that is part above and part below the film and again, the sipping rise is the norm.

Moving below the surface film there is an area where fish feeding on drifting nymphs still create a rise form which shows on the surface and which is sometimes called a **bulging rise.** It is probably the hardest to interpret as it is not uncommon for the dorsal fin to just break the surface if the nymphs being taken are close to hatching. Only careful and close observation will reveal the difference between this and a true sipping rise. A bulging rise can be created by a fish taking food anything up to a foot or slightly more under the surface depending on the size of the fish and the speed of thee take. The thing to look for here is how much water is displaced upwards by the rise. Fish moving close to the surface are likely to cause a big bulge with lots of water displaced whereas, when they are feeding deeper down, there is often only a flat spot created in the surface. For this reason the sip rise is usually associated with slower running water or very light ripple whilst, in fast water or a decent wave almost anything close to, in or on the surface is taken at speed with the fish breaking the surface even when nymphing. In these circumstances a trial and error approach must be adopted to decide whether it is floating or subsurface food being taken.

During mayfly hatches as well as some of the larger sedge

A slashing rise to a dry caddis on Corrib. Not a very big fish, about a 1 lb or so, but a lot of water disturbance just the same. I missed it!! Or did it miss me??

flies, fish will chase the fast swimming nymph or pupa up from the bottom so hard that they crash out of the water or at least throw water everywhere as they turn on the fly. This is known as a **slashing rise** and it is very hard to work out if the fish are on the ascending nymph, or taking skittering duns trying to take off, or egg-laying spinners buzzing across the surface, all of which can provoke **slashing rise** forms. I remember spending a whole day guiding during the mayfly hatch on the Test back in 2004, trying to work out what the fish were taking. They were literally turning somersaults in the air all day. It was late on in June and I was convinced they were either chasing duns taking off, or spinners still on the wing dropping bombs of eggs, but we struggled hard to catch a fish that day. Even a conventional nymph failed, I think because it could not be fished so as to come up vertically from the bottom. This day caused me to revisit what I now call the Swimming Mayfly Nymph pattern given later in the book. Interestingly other regular rods on the water I was fishing said this had been the norm right through that season with fish hardly ever taking anything but the ascending nymphs.

N B: There are no hard and fast rules here and the foregoing is merely a summary of the normal visual rise patterns you are likely to see. Some very large fish will simply open their mouths below a dun, emerger or spinner such that it literally falls into their mouth with the minimum of disturbance, so beware the tiny rise; it just could be a giant fish!

Understanding your Water and its Topography

I am going to look at rivers and lakes separately because fish behaviour differs slightly between the two.

1: RIVERS

Nearly forty years of working close to fish and fishermen as a river keeper, and more recently as a guide, has taught me just how important the surrounding countryside is. Indeed, some of my most enjoyable days guiding have been with fishermen who have wanted to learn how a river really works and who were prepared to sit and watch, or quietly walk the river between hatches, learning how the local topography affects the river. Probably the single most important and, sadly, most neglected part of a fly fisherman's skill, understanding the topography means understanding where you are going to find the fish in resting and, more importantly, in feeding mode. It can also dictate what, as well as where, some

Ballaglass Glen on the Isle of Man, a tumbling hill stream full of pocket pools and boulders. Fish can be caught by popping a fly into every nook and cranny. They will be small and fast but great fun.

insects and other food items will be found. In places where the current is squeezed into a tight food-rich channel, fish will take up station to feed, and every bend in the river, weed bed, rock, large tree root and fallen tree creates a potential fish lie. So too can a shady tree overhanging the water and dripping with beetles, mating flies and caterpillars to tempt our fish. Some of the lies created will be feeding lies, some will be for resting and others will be bolt holes for when danger threatens.

A typical falls pool on large rocky river. Well oxygenated water below the falls is ideal trout water and rocks like the ones in the foreground provide comfortable cushions, pockets, eddies and seams for the feeding fish.

These lies will vary depending on water level. They may be close together or some distance apart and, of course, there will be some areas that are just not good fish lies, but they are usually few and far between. Every type of river that holds trout, be it meandering slowly in flat farming country, or tumbling down steep, rocky slopes, will have its own particular types of lie. It is our job as fly fishermen to learn what makes a lie on our chosen water and approach it accordingly. Every yard of every river is individual and cannot be compared directly with any other, although there are many similarities.

Therefore it pays to understand what features contribute towards creating a good feeding lie and, as far as feeding is concerned, life for a trout is all about minimum input for maximum results. Fish, particularly large, mature ones, do no more than is necessary to obtain food. They will be looking for a feeding position that offers the following attributes; comfort, minimum energy use, nearby shelter and, most important of all, a regular supply of food. The best lie will hold the best conditioned fish, not necessarily the largest fish, and, when that fish is caught and removed, the next best conditioned fish will move in, often surprisingly quickly. River

One to the net from a deep pool on the Derbyshire Wye. The water in the pool above (behind) the angler drops into a deep pocket which tails out onto gravel shallows just below him. On the rising gravel bar below the angler, fish take up station to feed in cushions created by weed beds growing on the gravel. Just to the left of the angler is a steep drop off running for most of the length down the side of the pool and here the fish feed along the food-rich current seam this creates.

trout tend to be territorial. Almost every water has its myths about the big fish under the bridge, tree or similar lie. What this actually means is that it is the best lie on that particular stretch, but not necessarily always the same fish. Both submerged and emergent obstructions to the main flow, like weed beds and rocks as well as man-made structures like bridge piers, all create popular trout lies because they provide comfortable places for the fish. In front of each of these types of structure there is an area that I call a cushion where a fish can sit with minimum expenditure of energy and intercept the food as the river brings it to him. To the side and slightly downstream of these obstructions are yet more lies where fish take up station just on the quieter side of the current seams created by the obstructions. The fish then only have to move upwards and slightly sideways to intercept the food being carried by the faster current. By seam I mean the dividing line between two differing strengths of current. Spotting them takes a little practice but it is often possible to see frothy bubbles and items of flotsam travelling at differing speeds on the surface. The join between the different speeds of current is the seam. These seams can be created by obstructions as already stated, or simply by changes of depth.

Weirs and waterfalls, both natural and man-made, create cushions upstream, where fish like to feed, as well as well oxygenated pools, eddies and current seams downstream. Depending on the type of river there will also be gravel beds, islands or rock formations thrown up by the action of the current for quite a long way downstream creating wonderful trout habitat. This is why weirs are such a draw for both fish and educated anglers alike. In addition, especially on rivers with large bank-side alders and other trees, or where there are rocky areas of bank, you will often find eddies where the current is deflected by the root balls of the trees or by large rocks. Here you will have the usual seams but also an eddy where the current curls into the bank and rotates upstream before eventually rejoining the main flow. In an eddy, food is trapped, often for a long time, and fish will sit in an eddy, often facing down or across the stream, but always up-current, feeding hard.

A large, deep pool also creates numerous good lies, having various current seams and eddies within it. At the head of a pool there is often well oxygenated water created by water dropping down into the pool. Trout and grayling love this type of water because a lot of food is trapped here and they can be feeding on the drowned food deep down while hidden from predators, and from fishermen, of course. Well-presented nymphs are the order of the day here and time has to be spent finding the best way to get the flies down to these fish because of the mass of differing currents to be found. As the water levels out down through the middle of a pool there will be current seams and eddies to be searched, from the surface right down to the riverbed, while at the tail of the pool the currents will converge in one or more places as the bottom starts to lift, creating more rich feeding channels. Even in small, steep, rocky streams you will find a succession of small pocket pools, each containing some or all these elements in miniature. Each of these little pools will likely hold a fish or two. A stealthy approach, starting at the bottom and working up, will allow you to cover each of these pockets in turn.

On rivers that were utilised for irrigation in the past, such as the southern chalkstreams of England, you will find hatch pools controlled by lifting hatch gates. These provide all the features created by weirs but usually have very developed eddies in them. These eddies create a situation where the water returning from the eddy into the main stream is channelled underneath the fast cataract coming through the gates. Here there are fish-holding pockets right underneath the surging surface torrent where fish will feed completely invisible to us fishermen. Finding these hidden pockets is a special skill, honed with practice, and again a searching nymph is the tactic to use. Deep pools are not as easy to fish as they look and a lot of time is needed to learn how to read them properly. Finding the lies on your water will require time spent looking, not fishing.

One of my river guiding tricks, especially when I am with beginners and less experienced anglers, is what I call 'Bridge Leaning.' I encourage my anglers to lean on a bridge, tree, wall or whatever, and just look at the river for a few minutes. To study where the current flows fast or slow, where the rocks, weed beds, eddies, overhanging bushes and undercut banks are, as well as whether there any fish rising. I also show them the flies in the air

The River Dove as ir runs through Dovedale, Derbyshire. From this high vantage point it is possible to see the current seams created by the weir, rocks and weeds as well as the shady spots creating the various lies loved by trout and grayling.

and on the bushes, particularly looking under the leaves where upwing flies especially like to rest before transposing into spinners. Even spider's webs can give a clue as to what insects are about. I particularly look for upwings to see if there are any duns and spinners around thus giving a clue as to the likely size and colour artificial to use. If there are flies present in the air I point out the flight-patterns of different types of fly, as well as the various hatch stages of upwings that can be seen in the air and I often lift a stone or two to show what underwater food forms are around. Where appropriate I also seek out fry and other larger food items and point them out.

To see what is actually on the water at close quarters it pays to sit on the bank on the outside of a bend or on a low bridge over the main flow. This main flow can be found easily if you look for the foam and leaf litter lines present on almost every type of river. Foam lines are produced everywhere the river is constricted and speeded up, or where it drops over a weir and these foam lines are where most of the fly life, whether it be hatching or dying, as well as drowning terrestrials can be found. There are exceptions to this such as when mayflies are hatching because they can hatch from almost any type water and are not always on the water long enough to be channelled into the foam lines. It is obvious when this is happening as fish will be feeding all over the water, even cruising about in slower reaches, rather than just in the main feeding channels.

2: LAKES

While much of my working life has been on rivers, most of what I am saying here can be applied equally to lakes, llyns, lochs and loughs. In still waters, fish are tuned into depth, wind, contours, available oxygen, weed beds, rocks and other structure as well as trees and other bankside vegetation, all of which affect the food supply and consequently, the feeding habits of the fish. However, I have never found trout to be as territorial in still water as those in rivers, probably because they are at the mercy of the wind to bring the surface food to them or else they have to go searching for bottom living food items that can crawl or swim anywhere. It is not uncommon to catch fish of quite widely varying sizes in close proximity to one another. The *Caenis* feeding in June in Corrib

Looking across Lough Mask to the Partry Mountains on the western edge of the lough. These high, steep sided mountains indicate the deep water, up to 185 feet, to be found along that side of the lough.

is a prime example, when there are large pods of fish all feeding together. Always assuming you can catch them when they are feeding on the *Caenis* that is!

Now back to the topography. Steep sided V-shaped valleys usually suggest deep water e.g. Loch Ness, whilst U-shaped glaciated valleys suggest shallow water e.g. Tal-y-Llyn. Flat, lowland areas suggest shallow water e.g., Rutland Water and most of Lough Corrib. Steep banks on one side and shallow sloping banks on another indicate deep or shallow water respectively, and islands, rocky outcrops and other structure suggests possible fish-holding spots. This also holds good for larger, modern, man-made waters with the deeper parts normally being near dams. Look for submerged rocky outcrops of any kind as well as weed beds, because both habitats are full of food and, when near islands or the mainland, look for a drop-off where there is a sudden change in depth. Trout love these and will follow along the contours, feeding as they go. Also seek out incoming streams and rivers which are often a source of more oxygen-rich water and food from upstream. Keep an eye out for wide, shallow reaches of open water up to around twelve to fifteen feet in depth because there is almost always an abundance food in these places whereas the deeper water can be almost devoid of food at times, except for a few more specialised feeders that thrive there.

Looking south-east from an island in mid-Corrib showing the low ground to be found surrounding this part of the lough, indicating that the water is much shallower over the whole of this lower part of the lake.

If there is a good breeze or stronger wind acting on the surface it is possible to see wind-lanes and slicks where food is likely to be concentrated. Wind-lanes are relatively easy to spot, and food is frequently concentrated in the foam line along one or both sides. However, slicks are less easy to spot for the uninitiated. They are caused by vertically spiralling water currents created by the effect of the wind on the surface of the water. Within these slicks, either hot or cold surface water, according to the time of year, can be taken down and mixed with water of a different temperature deeper down, thus affecting its dissolved oxygen content. Slicks can be long and narrow, rather like wind lanes, or cover a wide area from the size of a tennis court to several football pitches. Insect food gets trapped in these revolving currents. Slicks usually give themselves away by having a different ripple pattern and a slightly glassy look but, at the risk of repeating myself, they are not easy to spot for the beginner. Taking a look from a high vantage point will often show them up. In the same way as boulders in a river create seams so islands in a large lake will do the same and it is common to find fish feeding downwind of a gap between islands where food carried by the wind has been channelled.

There is a general movement of the surface water downwind which sets up convection currents where cooler surface water

Almost flat calm on Corrib. Hard fishing conditions anywhere but stealthy boat work can pay dividends if you read the signs and get to know your water

sinks at the downwind end causing warmer water to rise at the upwind end of a lake or large bay. Fish will seek out either cooler or warmer water according to the dissolved oxygen levels that suit both them and their food and it is important to recognise this as there is an old wives tale that fish are always to be found at the downwind end. This is not always so, although it is a very common occurrence that they are found here. If conditions dictate they will favour the upwind end. Whilst dealing with the issue of wind it is important to point out that surface-feeding fish in lakes will feed into the wind if there is anything more than a very gentle breeze, so it is important to start at the upwind end of a drift and let the wind take you to the fish which may well be almost on the bank at the downwind end of the drift. In shallow lakes, like Lough Corrib, drifts over productive water can be very long in some shallower parts whilst over deep water the drifts tend to be shorter, except in the height of summer when fish move out over deeper water after daphnia. If there is no wind then they will often cruise and it is common to see fish cruising in an oval pattern or even a figure eight pattern, especially when buzzer feeding. Others will remain on station near favoured rocks or other lies, picking off the shrimp and other invertebrates, aquatic nymphs and emergers and occasional terrestrial flies as they find them.

If you prefer to fish at anchor then make sure you read all the signs first. You may well be miles from the fish if you do not. Pay particular attention to the depth of water you are anchoring in because, for much of the year, the most productive water will be less than twenty feet deep, with eight to fifteen feet being the best water to fish. It is important to find the right contours to anchor over as fish will often follow a set depth contour where their food is most prolific. It is also common to find rising fish travelling along a particular track on a regular basis rather than feeding haphazardly anywhere. In clear water finding the depth is relatively easy as you can see the bottom down to twelve feet or even more but, where the water is less clear, go by the changing colour of the water. The darker it looks, the deeper it usually is. However, be aware that sudden changes in the bottom substrate can cause confusion. For example, on Lough Carra in Co. Mayo, Ireland which is a shallow lake except for a couple of really deep holes, the bottom is mixed, with much of it being formed of marl, a light sandy colour, whilst the rest is covered in large weed beds which are very dark olive, giving the appearance of being much deeper when, in fact, they are both around the same depth.

A nice wave with plenty of foam lines on Lough Corrib

Even small, one to ten acre stocked trout fisheries have known hot spots created by such things as a deep pot hole, old stream bed, shallow spot, drowned tree roots or a freshwater spring.

WIND AND OXYGEN LEVELS

On larger, deeper lakes there is an extra element to consider in tandem with depth and that is the available oxygen. In extreme temperature conditions the dissolved oxygen levels are affected and water of differing temperatures and oxygen levels will stratify. Both the fish and their food will adjust their depth accordingly. In prolonged hot weather for instance, the upper layers of a lake will be oxygen-poor so the fish will be feeding deeper, at depths as much as thirty feet or more, creating the most challenging flyfishing conditions there are.

The same can be said for extremely still, cold conditions. Windy days with a good wave, much liked by both the Irish and Scottish lough fishermen, create oxygen-rich water right on the top and some of the best lough fishing is to be had on these days. However, the first time out on such a day can be daunting to the uninitiated and I well remember my first time on Lough Mask. It was just such a day and I left the seat numerous times as the boat dropped away off the top of a wave whilst we were moving about the lough. Upon remarking at the end of the day that I had been quite nervous at times, my guide Rod Tye, sadly no longer with us, simply smiled and replied that it had been a good wet fly wave. To be fair, we had had some nice fish on dry mayflies but it was a bit scary for the first time out.

As I prefer dry-fly and imitative nymph fishing on the loughs I tend to pick my days a little so that I can stalk or target fish more directly than when drifting fast before a good wind. The exception to this is when the fish are feeding hard on mayfly or caddis, when they will come well to a dry and it is a big enough artificial for me to see in the wave. There is nothing more exciting than seeing a large fish appear out of the wave to engulf your dry-fly. Pure fishing magic!

With time, you can learn to read all of the signs on your chosen water, but you have to put your hours in and spend time looking rather than fishing. Take half an hour out of every fishing day just to observe the water and its surroundings as well as the hatch patterns and you will become a more successful angler.

OBSERVATION IS THE KEY TO SUCCESS!

In this chapter I have tried to explain the various features that can create ideal fish feeding lies in both running and stillwater but, without being on *your* water with *you* I can only generalise. Now it is up to you. Using your powers of observation study the water you fish. Observe where the fish are rising or otherwise feeding as well as how and where the flies may be hatching. Note also where they lay their eggs and watch where the terrestrial insects drift in the current. Look for obvious seams, pockets, eddies; wind lanes on lakes and other features that may hold a fish and very quickly you will be able to read not only your water but you will also start to learn how to read other waters you visit.

Understanding the Larder

At the risk of being burnt at the stake for heresy I do not believe you have to be an entomologist able to recite the Latin names of the various flies you intend to imitate in order to be a successful fly fisherman, as some would have you believe these days. You really do not have to know your *Paraleptophlebia submarginata* from your *Serratella ignita*. By using your eyes you can imitate them without knowing their names. Size, colour and shape, along with the actual position of the fly in, on or under the surface film are the keys. However, I do believe that a simple knowledge of the life history and habits of the trout's food can make a vast amount of difference to your success rate and it is always good to see just what the various bugs and other food look like. Before moving on it is important to point out that trout are both aggressive and inquisitive by nature and there are times when they will 'taste' something they have never seen before or slash at something that intimidates them. I think this is why they sometimes take the garish lures we see in the tackle shops and can be caught on spinners of various shapes and sizes rather than being triggered into taking by a natural feeding urge.

So, let us take a look in the trout's larder to see what food he actually does eat. The answer to this may surprise many because it is just about anything that moves, be it the tiniest insect or a mouse. I liken a trout to a teenager. It is an eating machine but, if you have any experience with children, you will also know that one day they will be very fussy and only eat very specific things yet the very next day they will eat everything put in front of them and still be looking for more. So it is with trout. I make a habit of doing a stomach autopsy every time I keep a fish to eat. Over the years these checks have shown me that there are days when only one food item is present, say mayfly nymphs or perch fry, which shows very specific feeding. On other days, the contents are extremely varied, containing mixed items from the bed of the river or lake right up to the surface, showing a wholly non-selective feeding pattern while at other times it can be seen that there has been a pre-occupation with only one species all day, starting with the larva, moving on to the pupa, then to the emerger stage in the film showing a slightly more selective pattern. It is our job as fishermen to interpret the signs in order to work out what is actually happening. This is made much easier if we actually understand the hatch stages of the aquatic flies and the habits of the water bugs and terrestrials that we imitate.

The following list is not in any order of importance, nor wholly exhaustive, but merely shows the important food items that trout feed upon, starting from the bottom dwellers and then moving to the surface covering the various types of flies and other fauna whose life cycles we imitate.

- Shrimps, hog lice, corixae and water beetles.
- Damsel flies – larvae and adults.
- Upwinged flies.
- Caddis flies – also called sedge flies.
- Stoneflies and needle flies.
- Buzzers – also called chironomids, duck fly or non-biting midges.
- Terrestrials.
- Small fish, frogs, newts, crayfish and small mammals, all larger food items of particular interest to larger fish.

It is important to know that some of the items in this list are seasonal, like in our own larder, while others are available year round. It is also important to know the life cycles of many of these creatures on the list, particularly as certain stages are seasonal but still of extreme importance in the fish feeding pattern. The easiest way to explain this more fully is to take each of the above eight sections and expand them. I make no pretext of doing this in any scientific way or in order of importance, but merely to expand them as I view them, in the hope that it will be easy to understand and follow. I have picked out the ones that I think are of most interest to the fish and make no excuse for any not included. The behaviour of flies and their flight patterns as well as the seasonal appearance of terrestrial insects and other, larger food items, such as shoaling fry, all have a direct effect on trout feeding behaviour.

Identification is easy when they are this big and land on your arm

Even a simple thing like a herd of cattle or a tractor crossing the river can produce a feeding opportunity downstream, with dislodged shrimps and so on being carried by the current. I refer to all of these things as *triggers*. By recognising these triggers when they happen I have a better idea of knowing what is going on and, more important, when something is going to happen in advance, e.g., a fall of egg-laying spinners. Before certain species of upwings lay their eggs they fly upstream quite some distance in a swarm, 600 metres and more in my own experience, before finding a suitable egg-laying site, usually shallow, weedy reaches. I believe that trout pick up on these various insect movements as well and move to feeding stations accordingly.

On the river Test, I have witnessed trout following spinners upstream to a suitable vantage point just below the egg-laying shallow, ready to pick off the dying flies as they drift downstream. Some species of caddis migrate in the same way, laying their eggs in weedy shallows before drifting downstream to the waiting trout and grayling. When I see this upstream migration it is a trigger for me to move as well, for it is likely that only in these favoured egg-laying locations that feeding fish will be found. It is not only the adult flies that migrate of course. Some upwing nymphs and river caddis pupae drift a long way downstream as they make their way to the surface to hatch so, if there is upwing or caddis activity and fish are clearly feeding sub-surface, it could well be that they are taking these drifting nymphs or pupae.

On large lakes, the males of various chironomid species form huge swarms above the bushes in order to attract females for mating. These very visible and extremely noisy swarms are a

*Taking time
out to look into
the fly box*

trigger to me to stay out well into dark and find a suitable place to intercept the fish that will be feeding on the mated females when they return to the water to lay their eggs. In at least one species the males hawk across the water looking for females in the act of hatching. When they find one they mate before she takes wing. Sometimes many males attempt to mate with one female resulting in a mass of bodies called a cluster; a decent mouthful for a trout. On stillwaters even snails migrate at times, floating to the top where they are blown along by the wind before sinking again. Some fly-tyers have tried to copy this but I have never felt the need to do so.

A word of warning here: I am stressing the value of observation and watching for triggers but it is still easy to get caught out from time to time. I well remember one particular day back in the 1980s on the River Lathkill in Derbyshire during a 'Mayfly Weekend' when there were a number of the Duke's guests fishing. There were mayflies everywhere, the fish were rising hard all afternoon, yet no-one was catching anything. The first fish I netted was caught at around 5.00pm and I did a bankside autopsy straight away to see just what was what. The simple answer was that the fish had been stuffing itself on aphids all afternoon and there were only three mayflies, just at the back of its throat. It had switched to mayfly only minutes before being caught and, interestingly, all the guests fishing that day said the same thing had happened

Adult buzzers like this female found in the bushes gave the clue

An ejected natural pupa and the successful heavy buzzer that did the job

along about a mile of river. Fish were rising but not taking mayfly all afternoon, then a sudden change and the fish began taking mayflies everywhere. The lesson here is leave your blinkers at home. I certainly had mine on that day as it had been a real aphid year and I should have known better. Even so, I do not know what I would have given them anyway, as back then; I did not have an aphid pattern worth the name. I have never forgotten that day and now do my best to keep my eyes, ears and more particularly my brain open at all times whenever I am on the water.

One especially tricky time to get it right on a river is during the summer evenings when the light is dropping, usually spinner time, when there are blue-winged olives, pale watery olives and various caddis all hatching at the same time as various spinners are falling. There is little time to spare as darkness is coming very fast. You will only have a few minutes in which to find the right fly before it is too late to change, so, if you have not had a take from a feeding fish in three well-presented casts or so, change fly straight away because you have probably selected the wrong one. My first choice is usually an appropriate spinner, followed by a dry dun and then a caddis, unless there is a very obvious clue otherwise, but everyone has his own preferences. When you do get it right you can carry on fishing into the dark for a surprisingly long time, even fishing by ear if the river is not too noisy. It is amazing how you can hear a fish sipping in spinners if you really apply yourself.

Remember! A multitude of flies can be on the water at the same time so first identify what is there, then select appropriate imitations and, finally, select an order of play. When you fish this selection of flies do not waste too much time with any one fly if there is no immediate reaction to it. Change flies after say three, or at most five well-presented casts or you will soon run out of time. Being ignored is not an option as far as I am concerned. Once you have found the fly of the moment, make sure you still keep your eyes and ears open for the fish can change to another morsel very quickly. They are extremely fickle and it may be necessary to change your fly several times in the space of an hour or even less. The 'one fly man' does not fare well in these conditions and the man with a very full fly box needs to know what he has actually got in it.

Equally daunting are those days fishing on the lakes when no fish are showing on top to give you a clue as to what they are feeding on. Close observation of the surface for insect shucks, a check on any flies in the air and a close scrutiny of the bankside vegetation are the order of the day. Add a touch of local knowledge if you can glean some and you are in with more than a fair chance of selecting the right fly. In these circumstances you must give your selections a chance to work so make several drifts over likely holding water before you change flies but do not just leave the same flies on all day and hope. If you are missing fish on a regular basis it may be that you have not quite got the right fly and need to change colour or size, both of which can be major factors in the feeding pattern of the fish.

Part Two

FLIES AND TYING

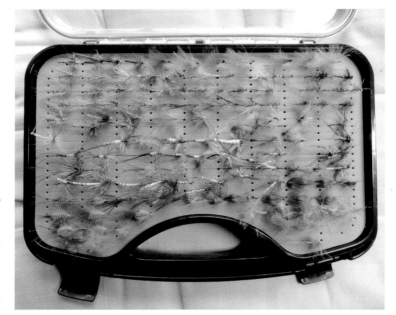

One side of
my Mayfly box
with patterns
covering
Emergers to
Spent flies.
Some patterns
are still 'work
in progress'

Stuck shuck
mayfly
emerger tied
by Phil White

On Buying and Tying Flies

Before expanding on the various food forms in more detail here are some thoughts on buying flies for the non-fly-tying reader of this book. There are many good retailers offering huge ranges of flies for you to buy. Every year sees yet more patterns being held up as the latest killers so, before you buy, take stock of what you think you will actually need. Here is a general look at flies for both rivers and stillwaters that might help. The chances are if you fish rivers you will need upwing and caddis imitations most of the time, with hawthorn, black gnat and daddy long legs at particular times. If you have a mayfly hatch then you will need some of these as well. On stillwaters you will be looking at similar terrestrials along with buzzers, caddis and some upwings if you are lucky enough to have olive or mayfly hatches. You will also need damsel nymphs and corixa patterns at times, as well as fry patterns on some waters. All waters have local favourites which you will also get to hear about. I do not intend to give long lists of patterns here as they are too subjective but at the end of each chapter on the food forms I have listed one or two patterns, some named specifically and others described more generally, that may help you make a selection. I have never found a fly fisherman who will not give information freely about his local water, be it a stocked fishery or a wild lough, and most decent tackle shops will know what works locally. Suffice it to say you need to check out local information. My advice is to make sure you have a good range of sizes in your boxes rather than a great diversity of patterns. Three sizes in three colours will do for most types of fly and carry both weighted and un-weighted subsurface flies. Fry patterns tend to be pretty specific and have little or no relationship to any of the brightly coloured lures that are available. That the latter work is not in contention but they are outside the scope of this book which I have deliberately aimed at wild trout fishing.

Take care to purchase from a reputable and repeatable source rather than buying the job-lot boxes offered in magazines or online these days and, at the risk of repeating myself, keep to a small number of tried and tested patterns, making sure you have them in a wide enough range of sizes and, in the case of nymphs, weights as well. If you are lucky enough to know a good fly-tyer then you can get exactly what you want.

For those who do tie their own flies there are patterns covering all the various food groups within this book. The fly dressings offered are all as tied by me for use in my own fishing and guiding. Some are as developed by me but some are merely variations of already successful patterns. Most of my own patterns contain elements gleaned from sharing ideas with a wide-ranging group of flyfishing fly-tyers, both professional and amateur alike, over very many years. I have not included patterns for frogs, mice or crayfish simply because I do not use them.

There is now a great diversity of hook sizing, where one manufacturer's size 10 can be another manufacturer's size 14, depending on the relationship between shank length, shape and bend, so make sure you are getting hooks that are the size you want, irrespective of the size given by the makers. All hooks I have quoted are given for size comparison, not brand preference. The only rule I have on hooks is that I avoid special price deals on hooks, and nylon for that matter, because, as they say in Yorkshire "You don't get owt for nowt." I do have my favourite hook makers and use their hooks because they do not let me down. The same goes for all my materials. Buy cheap and you buy twice.

Over the years I have tried all manner of shaped hooks and have come back to the good old fashioned shape for virtually all my own flies. The fly illustrated at the start of this chapter is one of my own designs from the very early 1990s. This fly produced the most confident takes from trout feeding on crippled mayfly emergers, I call them 'stuck shucks,' but I almost always failed to hook them, the fly coming out of the mouth every time – I think because it twisted as I struck due to the hook shank's pronounced bend. As a direct result of this I stopped using this hook in particular and bent hooks generally. I changed the fly onto a long shank York Bend hook, which is only slightly bent, and now get acceptably good results without the missed fish.

Shrimps, Snails, Hog Lice, Corixae and Similar Bugs

All of these are available to fish throughout the year and, apart from some moulting on a regular basis, they change little except in size. From a fly-tying angler's position I would say that, of these, the freshwater shrimp, corixa and water beetles are the most imitated. Fish do eat snails but I have not gone down that route although I have seen patterns by others.

THE SHRIMP

An abundant food item found in many trout waters, from the smallest brook to the largest lake, and, where present, much loved by trout and grayling. The shrimp is a crustacean, looking rather like a woodlouse that has been folded in half lengthways. There is a myth that shrimps swim on their backs and are always curled. Neither is true and five minutes looking at them in their natural surroundings will show that they swim at whatever angle

Two shrimps. Often seen paired like this. Could not separate them so shot them together

suits their purpose and when moving any distance stretch out straight, although they are a little hump-backed. The shrimp spends most of its life amongst the weeds, mosses and stones at, or near the bottom. The shrimp can reach up to an inch long and I recommend hook sizes 10 to 14 for imitations. In colour they are generally a grey-olive but, depending on the moult cycle, can vary from almost translucent to an orangey-olive. I have filmed shrimps taken during kick samples for club talks and have had several individuals in shot at once, each one being a different colour. For me the shrimp is a very important pattern when tackling deep feeding fish and I would never be without some imitations, especially in my river and small stillwater boxes.

THE HOG LOUSE

Much ignored in days past, this little bug is a staple part of the diet in rivers, particularly the slower reaches, as well as on stillwaters like

Ireland's Lough Corrib where I have found early season fish absolutely stuffed with them to the exclusion of all other food items. When they are feeding this way the fish are often very hard to tempt. Again, looking like the woodlouse, but not folded over as is the case with the shrimp, they are a mottled browny-grey in colour and very flat, which makes them a little difficult to imitate. They generally come in hook size 10 to 14 and I am experimenting with a pattern based on one by Dave Whitlock as I write this, although I suspect that some of the fish I have caught on dark olive shrimps have actually been feeding on hog louse. There is not a great deal of difference in the imitations and I have not included a separate dressing here.

THE CORIXA, WATER BOATMAN AND WATER BEETLE

In lakes, a short time spent looking into reasonably clear and relatively shallow water will expose just how many invertebrates there are swimming about that can be of interest to trout and other fish and you will see good numbers of both corixae (or lesser water boatmen) and other aquatic insects. At times, fish will become fixated on the corixa especially and feed on them subsurface for days, even weeks at a time, so it is as well to know what is in the water.

*Above:
Corixa. Not to
be confused
with the larger
carnivorous
water boatman
(below)*

I believe all of them to be very important food forms, particularly the corixa, which spends its time feeding around the stones and weed beds. I have caught both trout and carp on corixa patterns by stalking the weed beds in summer and targeting the fish that are cruising around picking the corixa off as they dart from place to place or pop quickly up to the surface to take on air. Behaving in a similar manner you will also see small aquatic beetles and I am quite sure they are

taken with the same relish. Most of the beetles are either black all over or black with brown backs. As well as the corixa there is the water boatman, a very similar looking but carnivorous beastie usually seen skating along on the underside of the surface-film looking for prey. Most beetles and corixae are in the 12 to 16 hook size range but there is one exception. This is the great diving beetle which can be as big as an inch long and 3/4 of an inch across in

Great diving beetle larva

its adult form, and at least two inches long as a nymph. This nymph is a serious and ugly-looking predator with nasty curved pincer jaws. It sits motionless among the stones and vegetation ready to pounce on passing small fish, tadpoles and the like, which it feeds on. Interestingly, when looking for suitable subjects to film and photograph I witnessed an epic battle between a beetle larva and a water boatman that were fighting over a tadpole that the beetle larva had caught. Slightly unexpectedly the water boatman won and swam off with the spoils. Did I have my cameras with me? No! Of course not!

Great diving beetle adult

LEECHES

More often thought of as a blood-sucking predator to be avoided, these are regularly eaten by trout and other fish. Much of the time they can be seen 'looping' along the stones but the leech also swims well and I have seen them swimming on numerous occasions. Large ones can easily stretch out to four inches or more and make a decent mouthful for a fish. They are olive-grey in colour and appear snake-like when swimming. I do not imitate them myself but there are a number of commercial patterns available.

SNAILS

These are eaten with relish by trout at some times of the year and even to the exclusion of most other food forms by some. I have found enough of the various types of snail in fish autopsies over the years to know that they will eat all the snails as well as various other freshwater molluscs, including the zebra mussel.

Ramshorn snail

SHRIMP

A must-have pattern on rivers and many stillwaters. Avidly taken by trout and grayling alike, this is one fly I would never be without, especially on rivers and small stillwaters.

Hook: Size 10 to 14 heavy wire such as Kamasan B175. I do not often use bent hooks, preferring standard-shaped patterns. Add more weight by winding lead or copper wire under the body or whipping layers to the top of the hook.

Body: Mixed seal's fur – I use 40% hot orange and 60% medium olive most of the time but vary this to have some more orange and some more olive. You can use dyed squirrel dubbing or various synthetics but I like the translucence of wet seal's fur.

Back: Olive or orange Bustard Thin Skin or olive or brown raffine (Swiss Straw) which swells very slightly when wet – open the strand and only use a narrow strip. Have a few tied with each coloured back.

Rib: Copper wire. Gold or other UTC wire colours also work well, so experiment to suit your water.

Legs: Body material picked out.

Fish this pattern dead-drift on rivers and with a slow figure-of-eight retrieve on lakes.

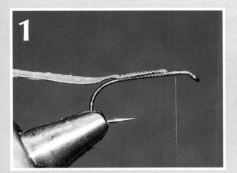

Set on thread and tie in flat lead.

Build up shaped body with flat lead. Cover with thread and varnish.

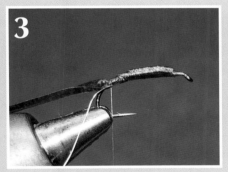

Catch in back material and rib wire.

Form the dubbed body.

Pull back over, tie down and rib. Form head. Whip finish.

Pick out the dubbing underneath.

CORIXA

There is a time in the summer when the main fly hatches occur very early in the morning or late in the evening. During this period daytime fishing consists mainly of imitating other aquatic water creatures such as corixa, often in mid-water.

Hook: Standard wet fly hook such as Kamasan B170 or B175 (heavier) size 12 to 14. Have some leaded and some unweighted.

Back: Cock pheasant centre tail (illustrated), or partridge back feather tied by the tip, or Orange Bustard Thin Skin.

Tag: Silver or UTC Opal tinsel coated with UV epoxy over to make the air bubble.

Body: Creamy dubbing – natural seal's fur, light Cahill Superfine, golden olive or cream Hemingway UV dubbing or fox squirrel belly.

Hackle: Brown partridge hackle stripped one side and one turn only. Set the fibres so they only project on either side. Pinch off any that are set upwards or downwards. The hackle represents the swimming legs.

Mainly a fly for stillwater, I fish this pattern on a floating line with a jerky figure-of-eight retrieve with frequent pauses. Beware of takes 'on the drop.' Concentrate your fishing near to weed beds, shallows and rocky areas where the fish will be hunting.

Set on thread and weight if needed.

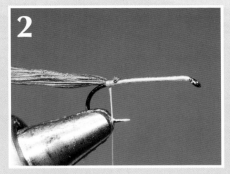

Catch in back material.

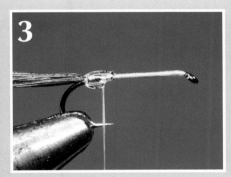

Form Tag and create UV bubble.

Form dubbed body.

Tie in hackle by tip. Two turns max.

Make neat head. Whip finish.

WATER BEETLE

Along with corixa, aquatic water beetles frequently figure in the stomach autopsies I carry out on any fish I keep to eat. I devised this pattern along with the corixa to fish when there is no obvious fly hatch or fish activity.

Hook: Standard wet fly hook such as Kamasan B170 or B175 (heavier) size 12 to 14. Have some leaded and some un-weighted.

Back: Natural pheasant tail for a brown beetle or dyed black cock pheasant tail, black Thin Skin, magpie tail (illustrated) or similar feather with a metallic sheen for a black beetle.

Tag: Silver or UTC Opal tinsel coated with UV epoxy to make the air bubble.

Body: Peacock herl or black ostrich herl as a variation.

Hackle: Black hen – one turn only. Use natural red for the brown backed version.

Head: Black thread, built up.

Again, a stillwater pattern fished in the same way as the corixa.

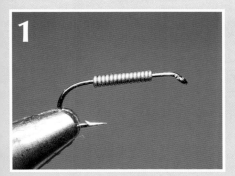

Weight hook - lead wire used here.

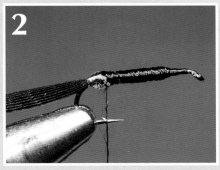

Cover lead with thread. Varnish. Tie in back. Form tag and UV bubble.

Tie in peacock herl and form body.

Tie in hackle by tip, stripped one side. Two turns.

Pull back over and tie off.

Make neat head. Whip finish.

**SHRIMPS, SNAILS, HOG LICE, CORIXAE AND SIMILAR BUGS –
Fly box suggestions for those purchasing their flies.**

Below are just a few from many patterns available from good
tackle shops and fly-tyers.

Shrimper – both olive and orange
Oliver Edwards' Shrimp
Red Spot Shrimp
Pink Shrimp – I don't know why it works but it does.
Chomper – an old pattern but still available from some fly dressers.
    This pattern comes in a huge range of colours covering corixa,
    shrimp and beetle patterns
Corixa
Black & Peacock Spider – for black beetles
Coch-y-Bonddu – for brown-backed beetles
Sawyer Killer Bug

Damsel Flies

Although mainly thought of as flies of stillwater, the damsel flies, and more particularly the demoiselles (identified by the black 'thumb marks' on the wings), are also found in the quieter margins of a great many rivers, stalking insects amongst the submerged stems of rushes and other vegetation. However, it is mostly in stillwater that the nymph and adult damsel fly are of serious interest to trout fishermen. The nymph is present all year round although for much of the time it is hidden in the weed beds and rushy areas where it stalks its prey. Fish will target them whenever they see them as they are a substantial meal but, when it is time to hatch – June to August in the UK, the nymphs travel to an appropriate rush bed or similar place where they crawl out before going through the hatching process to become adult. At this time the nymphs frequently expose themselves in open water, both close to the bottom and in many

A damsel nymph coming out to emerge. It was actually spotted swimming along the surface towards some rushes and intercepted for a quick photo shoot before being allowed to go on its way again.

cases swimming along the surface looking very much like a tiny fish. The fish feed voraciously on them at these times and a good damsel nymph imitation is an absolute must at this time of year.

There are times when the adult damsel flies are also taken. As newly-emerged adults, at which time most are a very pale watery olive, a blustery day will often see them blown back onto the water. Also, after breeding, the adults fall onto the water dead or dying and the fish will cruise around looking for the bodies and an appropriately coloured dry pattern can work. Fish will also target them when they are egg-laying. During a trip with the Fly Dressers' Guild to the Elan Valley in Wales back in the very

A newly hatched damsel hardening off. At this stage, on windy days, they can be blown into the water in large numbers when trout will target them.

late 1960s we fished a private club lake for a day. There, the red damsels were pairing up, landing on the stems of the short rushes and backing down to the surface for the female to deposit her eggs. Some of the resident brownies had fixed onto this and we could see the rushes moving as the fish stalked through them prior to launching themselves out of the water to intercept the paired damsels six inches and more from the water surface. Two of us spent the whole afternoon trying to find some way of imitating what was going on from our inadequate fly selections, but to absolutely no avail. If you fish a water where the fish target adult damsels it is always worth having an imitation tucked away for

Damsel flies 'Mating Heart'

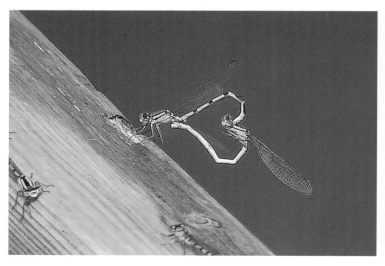

just such occasions with blue being the most common colour. It would pay to have one in pale olive as well to suggest the blown-in, newly hatched adults or the dying females. If you happen to fish an area where the red damsels are more prolific then go for red. Although I am working on a dry pattern – I do not like the current ones I have seen – it is not included in this book as it is not yet tried and tested.

I am sure that dragon flies, particularly the nymphs, figure in the trout's menu as well, but I have never bothered to imitate them because of their bulk and the difficulty in creating a good imitation. I believe that because they are slim, flies imitating damsel nymphs are much more likely to succeed, particularly those using mobile materials like marabou or Arctic fox as the tail material to imitate the sinuous swimming motion of the nymph.

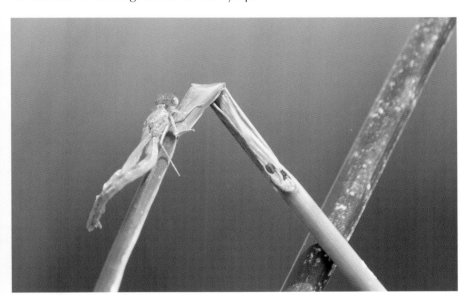

Newly hatched damsel drying out. At this stage they often get blown onto the water. Trout love them!!

LONG SHANK DAMSEL NYMPH

My best fish on this pattern was a wild brown trout on South Island, New Zealand, and he came up out of a weed bed to intercept it on the drop. The whole thing was as if in slow motion!

Hook: 2X or 3X long nymph hook size 10.

Eyes: Olive mono eyes – weighted variations include small bead chain, lead or tungsten dumb-bell eyes or lead, tungsten or brass beads. Have more than one weight so that you can get your fly down to search the depths off a floating line – it is amazing how mono leaders will hold even a weighted fly up.

Tail: Tips of olive goose herl.

Body: Olive goose herl.

Rib: Copper wire, olive wire or olive monofilament counter wound to strengthen body.

Wing case: Olive goose or similar tied with the tips laid back over the body nearly as far as the hook point.

Thorax: Olive marabou (illustrated) twisted and wound or a spiky olive dubbing like squirrel.

Hackle: Three open turns of olive dyed grizzle henny cock over thorax with top and bottom fibres removed or picked out dubbing fibres if hackle is not used.

A fly for slow searching around weed beds where the nymphs are hunting their insect and small fish prey. If you see the naturals swimming near the surface fish this fly a little quicker just under the surface.

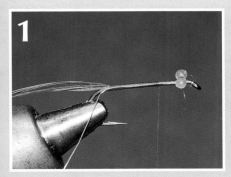

Tie in the eyes. Catch in tail herl and wire rib. Thread forward to thorax.

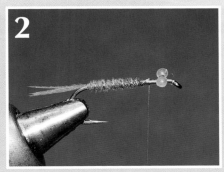

Form herl body and rib on opposite spiral.

Tie in wing case.

Tie in hackle if used. Form thorax.

Make 3 turns of hackle if used. Form wing case.

Form head. Whip finish.

SWIMMING DAMSEL NYMPH

This is a mobile fly, imitating the damsel nymph swimming, as they do when they approach an emerging site to hatch. At this stage the fish really go crazy for them if they are available in any numbers.

Hook:	Medium to short shank wet fly hook such as Kamasan B170, B175 or B160 size 10 – weighted under the thorax (or see eyes below) unless you want it to fish close to the surface – if so have some unweighted.
Eyes:	Olive mono eyes – other, weighted variations include small bead chain, lead or tungsten dumb-bell eyes.
Tail:	Olive marabou – not too much but tied long – there are numerous shades of olive to try, from nearly chartreuse to very dark olive, so experiment.
Body:	Wind the butts of the body marabou along the shank a turn or so.
Thorax:	Marabou as for body wound and tied off in front of the eyes.
Wing case:	Olive goose or pheasant tail a shade darker than the tail and body. Lay the tips back along the body to the end of the hook.
Hackle:	This is optional; I have some with and some without. Olive or olive grizzle hen or soft cock hackle – a couple of open turns wound through the thorax before the wing case is pulled over. An olive partridge hackle is also good but one turn only wound at the head before the wing case is pulled over.

Fish with a figure-of-eight retrieve at varying speeds until you find the speed the fish want on the day. Concentrate around weed beds or fish near the surface if you see the naturals swimming towards the bank or emergent vegetation.

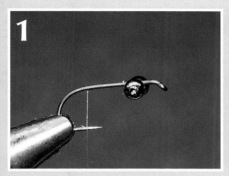

Set on the eyes. Thread to bend.

Tie in marabou tail.

Twist marabou butts and form body.

Tie in wing case.

Form the thorax.

Pull wing case over. Form head. Whip finish.

DAMSEL FLIES – Fly box suggestions for those purchasing their flies.

Below are just a few from many patterns available from good tackle shops and fly-tyers.

Any long-shank damsel patterns
be sure to get more than one shade of olive with at least light, medium and dark olive if possible – size 10 to 12.

Any short shank damsel patterns
with marabou or Arctic fox tails – same sizes and shades as above.

Upwinged Flies

Also commonly referred to as olives, mayflies or dayflies

These flies have been the subject of more written words than any other fly used by fishermen and yet it has been my experience that their life cycle is still little-understood by the average flyfisher. This lack of understanding can mean the difference between having a fish for supper and having a blank, and I have spent a lot of my time during guided days explaining what is happening on the river.

A stone-clinging nymph feeding on algae in the margins

The first thing to understand is that upwings of one kind or another can hatch at any time of the year, depending on weather and water conditions, so they are as important to grayling anglers as to trout anglers. The life-cycle of these upwings is quite simple. From the egg a nymph hatches and starts to grow. Different species of nymph require different living conditions and they are often classed according to where they live. Some examples are: burrowing nymphs such as mayflies (*Ephemera danica*); slow-moving moss-dwellers like the blue-winged olive (*Serratella ignita*); stone-clingers like the march brown (*Rhithrogena germanica*) and yellow may dun (*Heptagenia sulphurea*) that cling to rocks in fast rivers or rough lake shores and more agile nymphs like most of the river olives (*Baetidae* and others) and lake olives (*Cloëon simile* and others) that live amongst the weed beds and swim freely, often very fast. It is these special requirements that can dictate how and where the adult females lay their eggs, of which more later. As it grows, each nymph goes through a number of moults, or instars. During this growing period the wings develop until the fly is ready to hatch. Indeed, it is possible to tell how close a nymph is to hatching by looking at the size of the wing case. It will be both

An agile swimming nymph from Corrib

large and dark coloured close to the time for hatching. Once ready, the nymph makes its way to the surface and, in due time according to conditions, punches its way through the surface film, splits the outer skin, or shuck, at the thorax and the adult fly emerges onto the water as a dun, or sub-imago. As soon as the wings are dry and hardened off, the dun flies to the bank and takes shelter in nearby vegetation where it hardens off even more, ready for the next stage in its adult life. During this initial drying time the dun floats on the surface looking for all the world like a little yacht. Its wings are set so that if there is any breeze the fly faces into the wind ready for take-off.

The **flight of the dun** should be noticed as it is a trigger feature, telling you that duns are hatching even if you cannot see them on the water. The duns fly rather clumsily with the body almost vertical, often making two or three attempts to take off, and the direction of flight is always upwards towards land unless there is a strong breeze forcing them to stay low over the water. Look closely under the leaves of bankside trees and bushes or in dense grasses and rushes and you will see them. At this stage the adult

A mayfly dun hangs under a nettle leaf ready to transpose into a spinner

growth is not quite complete and, to me, the dun stage is a form of pupal stage. The wings are opaque, the tails are short, no more than the length of the body, and the body colours are drab shades of olive. Now it is possible to tell the difference between the sexes. The females have their eyes on the sides of their heads whilst the males' are set more on the top of their heads. In all but the smaller flies it is also possible to see the male organs, sometimes referred to as claspers, under their tails. After a while, from minutes with the *Caenis*, up to several days in some conditions, the fly will moult another skin and become a spinner, or imago. If you are lucky you will see this last moult and it is well worth watching as it is one of nature's little wonders.

After much shimmying and body-twitching the thorax splits and the fly gradually emerges from this final shuck in all its sparkling glory. The wings are clear and glistening whilst the body is polished and brightly coloured, especially in the females, which may be red, cream, yellow or orange whilst the tails, particularly those of the males, are up to twice the length of the body, even more in some species. The long front legs of the males are now very noticeable, frequently being held off the ground, pointing forward. It is only at this stage that the flies can breed.

The **flight of the spinner** should also be understood as it is again a trigger as to what is on and over the water. The male spinners will go into a mass **display flight** in an appropriate place that can be species specific – some prefer open grassland, others in the lee of the overhanging tree

Male caenis dun transposing into a spinner – this took a total of ten minutes from landing

Male mayfly spinner resting under a leaf prior to commencement of the dance – note the long front legs held aloft and the long tails

canopy and yet others, such as the mayfly (*E. danica*) over the top of high trees if the wind allows. Very few actually display over water although there are one or two exceptions, particularly the iron blue dun. In the right conditions it is possible to see hundreds, if not thousands of males displaying. The flight pattern, often referred to as the dance, is always in the form of vertical sweeps of from a couple, to dozens of feet upwards, followed by a controlled parachuting fall, and is repeated almost *ad infinitum*. On windy days these dances are often very intermittent with the flies diving into the bushes when it blows hard. If the weather is sunny the wings of the spinners sparkle and shine as they dance. As soon as they are ready to breed the females join the male dance where they mate, usually, but not always, in flight. After mating the males will go back to the dance until they are completely spent, when they drop wherever they are, and die, sometimes on water but not always. For this reason the male spinner is less often imitated than the female. The females go to the water, for this is where they lay their eggs, and, after egg-laying, they die.

The **flight-pattern of the female spinner** also needs to be understood and there are two main types of egg-laying and pre-egg-laying flight to consider. The first is the 'bombing run' used by the mayfly and quite a few others. The female spinner carries her body more or less horizontal and flies much more strongly than the dun, quartering the stream or chosen area of the lake dipping down periodically to lay a batch of eggs. As she flies she extrudes some eggs which collect in a mass on the lower abdomen. When she dips to touch the water the eggs wash off and sink immediately. She then flies to another spot and repeats this process, extruding eggs as she flies, all the time getting weaker and weaker until, finally, she will get trapped in the surface film, still laying eggs until she dies. This final dying stage is known as the spent stage when the fly lies flat on the surface. At this stage the flies are often referred to as 'spent gnats' or just 'gnats' whether they be male or female. The area where the eggs are laid is non-specific in that the spinner simply flies hither and thither, laying batches of eggs in a fairly haphazard fashion, leaving the eggs to hatch wherever they come to rest. I have seen mayflies laying eggs in puddles, on wet roads near rivers and even on my wet car.

On rivers, mayfly spinners drop on the water anywhere and are carried downstream by the current. Fish will feed avidly on them, often

Female mayfly spinner resting under a leaf prior to the dance – note the more creamy body and lighter markings

to the exclusion of any other food forms. Look for main current flows when fish are spinner-feeding and you will find the majority of the action, for the flies get funnelled into these main flows as the river runs through bends, narrows and between stones or weed beds. Also look for back eddies where the flies are often trapped by the circulating current, a favourite lie of big brown trout. Fish know this and take the necessary action to place themselves in the best position to take maximum advantage. As you spend more time on a particular stretch of river you will become accustomed to the best feeding zones such as the outside of bends where fish are often feeding almost nose to tail late in the summer evenings, or where a tree root or rock creates a sudden concentration of the flow. Spinners are equally important on any lake that has hatches of upwinged flies such as mayfly, pond olives or lake olives. On the large mayfly loughs of Ireland for instance, fishing the 'spent gnat' involves sitting around in a boat until the female flies come away from the trees to lay their eggs in the open water downwind, where hopefully the fish will come up to feed on them. Because it is often windy on the loughs the males are also frequently blown onto the water, usually in the late evening, and the fish

The long and short of it! Mayfly and caenis spinners both on the water together.

will take these male spinners as well as, or even instead of, the females. The same can be said for any lake with a mayfly hatch. Just place yourself downwind of a mayfly dance site and wait for the fly to come onto the water. At times the downwind shoreline is thick with dead and dying fly and this can be a real hot spot providing memorable spinner fishing. In the same way both lake and pond olive spinners can provide really good fishing when they fall.

The second type of egg-laying flight is much more specific and concerns flies that need special conditions for the nymphs to succeed. These spinners fly upstream, often in huge swarms to a specific area before egg-laying. Some carry 'bombs' of eggs whilst others, the *Baetis* group in particular, actually alight and crawl down underwater to lay their eggs below the surface. Again the flight is stronger than that of the dun but, in the case of those which extrude their eggs in a ball, they carry their bodies vertically with the tails curved forwards making them look rather

Not all spinners land spread-eagled. This one is on its side and I have seen them on their backs as well

like upside down question marks, a real clue as to what is about to happen. Over the years, I have followed swarms of these 'question marks' up to six hundred metres upstream to a suitable weedy shallow where they have laid their eggs. More importantly, I have also followed fish moving upstream at the same time to find the only rising fish anywhere on the river feeding in the slightly flatter water immediately below the egg-laying site. Knowing that this could and would happen late in the day has saved me from many an otherwise blank hot summer's day guiding on a dry-fly-only stream. On waters I know well I actually assume that fish will be feeding in this way and make sure I get to a favourite egg-laying site first. Spend just one day on a river watching, rather than fishing, and you will see duns hatching and spinners egg-laying at the same time and within a very short period of time you will learn to recognise all of the triggers I have mentioned.

HERL BODIED NYMPH

I like herl as a body material and dress these nymphs to give me slim imitations with a little translucency rather than the more bulky commercial patterns generally available. By ringing the changes with different feathers a wide range of colours can be tied.

Hook: Size 10 to size 20. Standard dry-fly, medium weight, and heavy weight hooks offering a variation in fly weight. Extra weight can be added with both copper and lead wire.

Tail: Tips of body-herl, hackle fibres, partridge hackle fibres or summer duck flank feather fibres. The latter two are for nymphs with noticeably speckled or spotted tails like the blue winged olive, lake olive and several others.

Body: Herl from cock pheasant tail, goose shoulder feather, summer duck and mallard flank, all natural or dyed.

Rib: Fine copper, gold, silver wire as well as other colours of UTC wire. I also use the following thread colours for a rib instead of wire: orange, olive, yellow and claret.

Wing case: Grey duck primary, dark mottled turkey tail, pheasant tail and similar dark fibres or a dark partridge back feather tied in by the tip and pulled over.

Thorax: Squirrel body or rabbit dubbing both natural and dyed.

Hackle: One turn of partridge body or back hackle pulled back and under or a few fibres of the dubbing picked out.

N.B. By tying a heavier body and hackle as well as a longer tail a wide range of naturals can be imitated.

Fish dead-drift with an occasional lift on rivers and with a figure-of-eight retrieve on lakes. Watch for takes on the drop, especially when fishing on lakes.

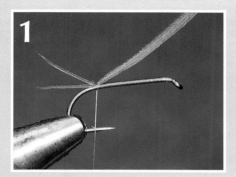

Tie in tail material.

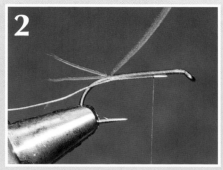

Catch in rib. Take thread forward to thorax.

Form body and counter wind rib.

Tie in wing case material. Form dubbed thorax.

Strip hackle one side, tie in at tip, wind two turns.

Pull wing case forward, tie in. Form head. Whip finish.

DUBBED BODY NYMPH

Probably the best-known dubbed-bodied nymph is the Gold Ribbed Hare's Ear Nymph which, in its simplest form, has the tail, body and thorax made up of hair from a hare's ear, ribbed with oval or fine flat gold tinsel, without any extra appendages like hackles or wing cases and has been catching for centuries. Fished in the surface film I look upon it as the first emerger pattern. By varying the natural and dyed furs available today a wide range of colours can be tied up and the following is the basic dressing I use.

Hooks: Size 10 to size 20. Standard dry-fly hooks, medium weight hooks, short shank hooks and heavyweight hooks. This will offer a wide variation in weight and you can add lead if required.

Tail: Squirrel or similar guard hairs.

Rib: Oval gold tinsel, copper wire or other colours of UTC wire to suit.

Body: Hare, squirrel or rabbit dubbing – natural or dyed.

Wing case: Grey duck primary, dark mottled turkey, pheasant tail and similar dark fibres or a dark partridge back feather tied in by the tip and pulled over.

Thorax: Squirrel or rabbit dubbing with plenty of guard hair – natural and dyed.

Hackle: Picked out guard hairs or one turn of brown partridge hackle pulled back and under.

N.B. By tying slim nymphs with short tails and much stouter nymphs with longer tails you can imitate all the natural shapes taken by upwinged nymphs.

Fish as for herl-bodied nymph.

Tie in the tail fibres.

Tie in ribbing wire.

Form dubbed body.

Counter wind rib. Tie in wing case.

Form dubbed thorax.

If using hackle tie in and wind now. Pull wing case over, whip finish

SWIMMING MAYFLY NYMPH

This has been developed from the swimming damsel nymph and anyone who has seen the nymph swimming will appreciate why I use the long marabou tail rather than the more traditional long shanked hook that nymphs are more commonly seen tied on.

Hook: Size 10 or 12 medium to heavy wire Kamasan B160, B175 or similar.

Head: Black tungsten or copper bead.

Tail: Grizzly marabou/Chickabou dyed tan or lightly bleached to turn the black bars dark reddish brown.

Body: Light cahill or pale morning dun Superfine dubbing or Hemingway's UV dubbing in golden olive.

Hackle: Brown partridge stripped one side, wound two turns and pulled down.

Wing case: Cock pheasant tail fibres pulled over bead and tied off with a large head. Leave the tips protruding back over the body when you tie it in.

This fly is fished dead drift to sink and then lifted smoothly to the top like an ascending nymph, before re-casting. Quite a lot of takes come on the drop or before the lift presumably because of the mobile nature of the tail. N.B.. Check your fishery rules as not all river fisheries will allow this one.

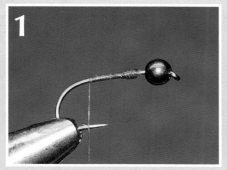

Thread bead on hook. Take thread to bend.

Tie in tail marabou.

Twist marabou stem and form body

Tie in wing case.

Dub thorax. Two turns of hackle. Tie off.

Form head in front of bead, pull wing case forward and whip finish.

LOOP WING OLIVE EMERGER

The pattern I use when the fish are feeding on newly emerging nymphs just breaking through the surface.

Hook: Fulling Mill Down Eye Dry, TMC 103BL or similar hook in sizes 14 to 22.

Tail: A fairly large bunch of summer duck flank. This represents the shuck.

Body: The butts of the tail fibres wound one third up the hook.

Rib: The tying thread. I normally use yellow, orange, olive and claret.

Wing Loop: Three CDC feathers tied in behind the thorax and then pulled over as a loop wing. Use two feathers only below size 18.

Thorax: Superfine dubbing in appropriate shades as follows: pale morning dun with yellow thread, golden olive with orange thread, olive with olive thread and grey with claret thread.

Fish this pattern on rivers and on any lakes where there is olive activity. I twitch the fly occasionally to simulate the fly struggling out of its shuck.

Tie in tail fibres over point and bind down to bend.

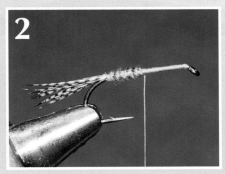

Wind butts of tail fibres to bend. Tie in. Wind thread forward as a rib.

Catch in three CDC feathers

Form dubbed thorax.

Pull CDC feathers forward to make loop. Whip finish

LOOP WING MAYFLY EMERGER

For those days when the fish have fixated on the newly exposed transition nymph hanging in the film in the act of breaking through the thorax, wings still partly trapped in the nymphal shuck. Some days this can last several seconds, enough time for the fish to take them without rushing. The fly floats on the CDC bubble with the tail awash.

Hook: Fulling Mill down-eyed Dry or TMC 103BL size 10 or 12.

Tail: Light cock pheasant tail, at least seven or eight strands, tied long to suggest shuck.

Body: The butts of the tail fibres wound over the rear third of the hook and ribbed with the tying thread.

Thorax: Pale morning dun Superfine dubbing.

Wing Loop: Three olive or natural CDC feathers and one small summer duck feather as a cover.

N.B. As with the Hatching Mayfly dun I am experimenting with natural red fox tail instead of pheasant tail for the tail (shuck) and am having good results.

Fish on both rivers and lakes, wherever there is a mayfly hatch. Again, I twitch this fly to suggest life.

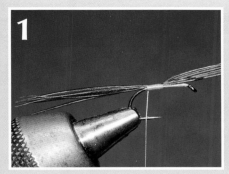

Catch in tail fibres mid hook and take thread to bend.

Wind herl butts to bend. Tie in. Rib thread back.

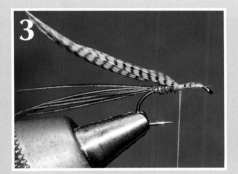

Catch in summer duck feather.

Catch in CDC feathers.

Dub thorax then loop both CDC's over.

Pull Summer Duck over top of loop. Form head. Whip finish

HATCHING OLIVE

A pattern for those days, usually cool and damp, when the fly is slow hatching and travels a long way with the shuck still attached. Whilst the shuck is still attached the fly cannot take off. The fish seem to know this and fix on this stage of the hatch. This pattern is a reduced version of my Hatching Mayfly.

Hook: Short shank dry-fly hook such as Fulling Mill down-eyed Dry-fly or TMC 103.

Tail: A fairly heavy bunch of summer duck flank fibres tied at least as long as the hook.

Body: The tail butts wound half-way along the shank.

Rib: The tying thread – see illustration. I use yellow, orange, olive and claret.

Thorax: Superfine dubbing in appropriate shades. Pale morning dun with yellow thread, golden olive with orange thread, olive with olive thread and grey with claret thread. Try your own colour combinations as well.

Hackle: Cock hackle of appropriate colour. I use light and medium duns or pale ginger. The hackles are wound in open palmer over the whole of the thorax area. I clip a V out of the underside of the wound hackle to make the fly sit low on the surface as the natural does.

Wing: CDC bunched or whole feather tips (illustrated) if preferred. Lay the wing back a little as if it has only just broken free of the shuck.

A fly for rivers as well as lakes with an olive hatch. I twitch this fly to suggest the fly is struggling to free itself from the shuck.

Tie in tail fibres 1/2 way down. Thread to bend.

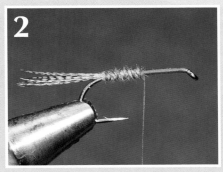

Wind butts to bend. Tie in and rib forward.

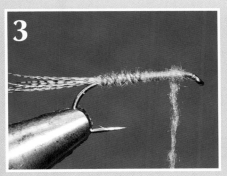

Dub thorax and then one turn back.

Tie in hackle and dub back down to shuck.

Palmer hackle down and rib thread to front.

Tie in wings. Form head. Whip finish.

HATCHING MAYFLY

An imitation of the mayfly in the act of hatching, with the wings already free and drying but the shuck still attached. On cool days the act of eclosion can take quite some time, I have filmed mayflies taking nearly thirty seconds for the fly to break completely free of the shuck and the fish seem to fix on this stage readily. This pattern has been by far the most successful of my nine 'hatch stage' patterns and was developed as far back as the late 1970s. The set of the wing has been changed slightly, laid back a little more than the original's upright post, but it still keeps on catching.

Hook: Fulling Mill Down-eyed Dry or TMC 103BL size 10 or 12, both of which are slightly shorter than modern standard dry-fly hooks.

Tail: Light cock pheasant tail, at least seven or eight strands, tied long to suggest shuck. Golden pheasant undertail also works well.

Body: The butts of the tail fibres wound one third up the hook and ribbed with the tying thread.

Thorax: Pale morning dun Superfine dubbing.

Hackle: Grizzle dyed light-olive.

Wing: Natural or light-olive dyed gold bull elk mixed with moose body hair to suggest the veins in the wing. Dyed light-olive bucktail also works well if elk is not available.

Head: Butts of wing fibres trimmed proud over the hook eye.

N.B. At the time of writing this I have started experimenting with a bunch of natural red fox tail for the tail (shuck). This seems to work just as well.

A fly for rivers and lakes wherever there is a mayfly hatch. Another fly I twitch on the surface and sometimes even slide it several inches across the surface to suggest the fly is stuck in the shuck.

Thread half way, tie in tails, thread to bend.

Wind butts to tail and catch in.

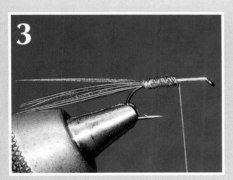

Rib thread forward over herl.

Dub the thorax and take two turns back down. Catch in hackle and dub back down hook.

Wind hackle and rib through with thread.

Tie in wings and form head. Whip finish and trim wing butts and hackle V.

SHUCK STUCK MAYFLY DUN

Both early in the hatch and, to a lesser extent right through the hatch, I have noticed a lot of crippled duns on some days that cannot seem to shed their nymphal shuck because their tails are trapped. The shuck rolls up at the tail of the fly instead of sliding neatly away as it should, leaving them stranded, struggling on or in the surface film.

Hook: Size 10 or 12 3X long Living Larva hook or 2x long dry-fly hook TMC 5212.

Tail: Grizzly marabou dyed tan or lightly bleached to give ginger bars.

Body: Rear half grizzly marabou spun and wound on followed by pale morning dun Superfine built up a little at the thorax.

Hackle: Grizzle dyed light-olive wound over the whole of the dubbing in open palmer. Trim out a wide V in the underneath hackle so the fly sits low.

Wings: Natural or light-olive dyed gold bull elk mixed with moose body, or natural brown bucktail or summer duck tied as a bunch wing.

Head: The wing butts clipped to leave a short bunch over the hook eye.

Good on rivers and lakes. I devised this pattern for a very specific set of circumstances but it has proved itself for much more general use over the years. Give this fly a little movement to simulate it struggling to get rid of the shuck.

Take thread to bend. Catch in marabou feather by tip.

Twist marabou stem and form shuck.

Dub thread. Form thorax. Tie in hackle.

Dub down body. Wind hackle and rib through with thread.

Tie in wing. Form head and whip finish.

Trim wing butts and wide V in hackle.

UPWINGED DUN

I have been using this pattern successfully for many years now and developed it down from my mayfly range. It contains elements of the thorax style of fly together with CDC wings.

Hook: Standard dry-fly hook such as Kamasan B400, TMC 100 or 103.

Tail: Small bunch of four or five summer duck fibres tied short, equal to gape of the hook at most.

Body: Two turns of the tail butts wound on before dubbing the rest of the body with Superfine dubbing in appropriate shades. Pale morning dun with yellow thread, golden olive with orange thread, olive with olive thread and grey with claret thread. Try your own colour combinations as well.

Thorax: Same dubbing as body.

Hackle: Cock hackle of appropriate colour. I use light and medium dun or pale ginger. The hackles are wound in open palmer fashion over the whole of the thorax area. I clip a V out of the underside of the wound hackle to make the fly sit low on the surface as the natural does.

Wing: CDC, bunched or whole feather tips if preferred. For waters where there are hatches of march browns or other upwinged flies with speckled wings use summer duck flank as a bunched wing.

On rivers fish dead drift as any normal dry fly. Use the olive, yellow and orange thread versions on lakes where there are olive hatches.

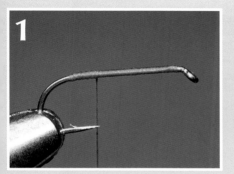

Thread to bend then forward to hook point

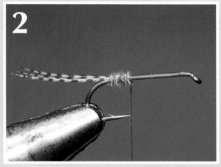

Tie in tail fibres. Thread to bend. Wind butts to bend. Rib over with thread.

Dub body forward then one turn back.

Catch in the hackle and dub back to hook point.

Palmer hackle and rib through with thread.

Tie in CDC wing. Form head. Whip finish. Trim V in hackle.

NO HACKLE DUN

This is my take on a Marc Petitjean pattern and I seek no credit for it. I use this when small duns are on the water and my other dun patterns do not work. As it sits very low I cannot make up my mind if it is taken for a dun or an emerger, but it is taken with relish on its day.

Hook: Standard Dry-fly, TMC 103BL or similar hook in sizes 14 to 22.

Tail: Small bunch of four or five fibres of summer duck flank or cock hackle but tied short, equal to the gape of the hook at most.

Body: Dyed CDC twisted and wound Petitjean style (see tying instructions) – I use pale yellow, golden olive, light olive, olive dun, grey and dun or tan.

Wing: CDC bunch in dyed light dun, natural khaki or natural grey – no stems in the wing. I always have some of each as different naturals have different colour wings.

Fish this fly dead-drift on rivers and lakes where there is an olive hatch and, in smaller sizes, for caenis.

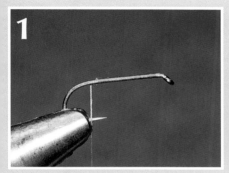

Tie in tail fibres at the bend.

Catch in CDC feather by tips.

Twist feather anti clockwise and wind to form body.

Trim butts off CDC feathers and pull the fibres downwards.

Tie in CDC so no stems are included.

Form head. Whip finish. Trim wing fibres if necessary.

F-DUN

The F-Fly by Marjan Fratnik is so well-known today that it needs little or no introduction. I have merely added tails and set the wing a little more upright to make it a little more like a dun. I tend to use it only in small sizes but I have seen people use it as big as a mayfly with some success. The wing on the original F-Fly is made with the tips of whole CDC feathers but I prefer to use bunches tied in a specific manner to do away with the stems. See step-by-step instructions.

Hook:	Standard dry-fly hook such as Kamasan B400, TMC 100 or TMC 103BL. sizes 16 and smaller.
Tail:	Small bunch of summer duck flank fibres or cock hackle fibres no longer than the gape of the hook.
Body:	Tying thread – orange, yellow, olive and claret are my normal colours. Also stripped peacock quill dyed in orange, yellow, olive and claret.
Wing:	CDC fibres bunched without the stems.

Fishes well in small sizes on streams as well as lakes where there is olive or, in smaller sizes, caenis activity.

Catch in tail at the bend.

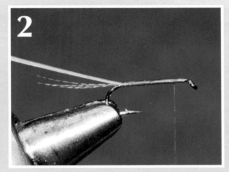

Catch in body quill. Take thread forward.

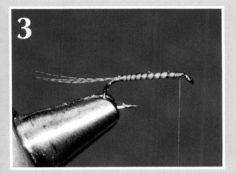

Varnish thread base and wind quill body.

Take 2/3 CDC feathers and trim off butts - see pic.

Pull fibres down and tie in with no quill in wing.

Form neat head. Whip finish. Trim any long fibres.

ACTIVE MAYFLY DUN

I devised this to represent the newly hatched dun sitting on the water prior to its first flight as I was not satisfied with the existing patterns on the market. It first saw light of day on the Lathkill, a Derbyshire limestone stream that is incredibly clear and very slow in parts, and it completely out-fished everything else used at the time. The trimmed 'V' is very important!

Hook: Standard dry-fly hook size 10 or 12.

Tail: Four or five fibres of cock pheasant tail about the length of the shank.

Body: Two turns of the tail fibre butts followed by pale morning dun Superfine dubbing. Use olive Superfine instead if you are in an area where the darker Ephemera vulgata is present.

Rib: The pheasant tail fibres are ribbed with the dubbed Superfine prior to the building of the body.

Hackle: Grizzle dyed light olive wound palmer along half of the body. Trim out a large V underneath so the fly sits low on the water.

Wing: Natural or light olive dyed gold bull elk mixed with moose body hair to suggest the veins in the wing. Dyed light olive bucktail also works well if the elk is not available. If a feather wing is preferred then summer duck flank tied as a bunch wing is also excellent.

Head: Butts of the wing fibres clipped proud over the hook.

I usually fish this pattern dead drift as the newly hatched dun tends to be fairly still for the drying period. However, on colder days I move the fly a little as the naturals take quite a time taking off, frequently 'stumbling about' on the surface before getting airborne.

Tie in tail material above the point. Thread to bend.

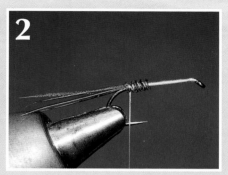

Wind herl butts to bend. Catch in.

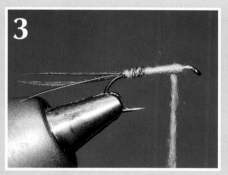

Dub thread, rib herl then form body. Two turns back down body.

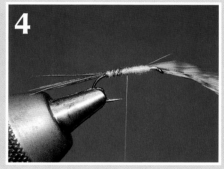

Catch in hackle and dub back to hook point.

Palmer the hackle. Wind thread forward through it.

Tie in wing. Whip finish. Trim wing butts. Trim V in hackle.

DANCING MAYFLY DUN

On some days, particularly cooler days, the newly emerged mayflies make several attempts to get airborne, skittering along the surface as they do so, and the fish lunge after them. This fly is also good for those days later in the hatching period when the fish are jumping after airborne duns rather than taking the flies on the water in the conventional way.

Hook: Size 10 or 12 dry-fly hook.

Tail: Cock pheasant tail as long as the body.

Body: Two or three turns of the tail butt fibres ribbed with pale morning dun Superfine dubbing then dubbing for the rest of the body.

Hackles: Light olive dyed grizzle cock palmer wound heavily over two thirds of the body with a small summer duck flank wound in front of the palmered hackle.

Cast the fly beyond the fish and then skitter the fly by lifting the rod whilst drawing on the line with the line hand so that the fly comes up onto the plane, skimming along on its hackle tips. Speed is important here with a slow draw needed some days and a faster pull on others. Sometimes just a short draw will work and other times long steady ones. Every day is different.

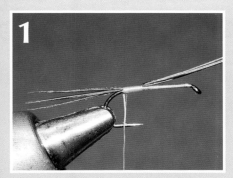

Catch in tail fibres at hook point and take thread to bend.

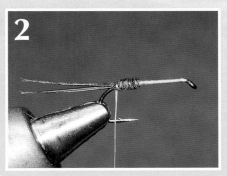

Wind butts to bend and catch in.

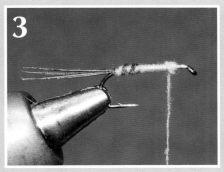

Rib herl with dubbed thread and then form body. One turn back down body.

Catch in hackle and dub back down body.

Palmer the hackle down body and rib with thread.

Tie in Summer Duck hackle by tip. Two turns. Form head and whip finish.

BLOWN OVER MAYFLY DUN

On windy days it is common to see a lot of newly hatched duns blown over with one or both wings trapped in the surface film. This pattern is tied to represent a dun trapped with one wing in the film. This was developed from an idea put to me by Mike Brookes who had been experimenting with my then-new One-Up Spinner pattern on the River Lathkill back in the early 90s.

Hook: Standard dry-fly hook size 10 or 12.

Tail: Four or five fibres of cock pheasant tail about the length of the shank.

Body: Two or three turns of the tail fibre butts followed by pale morning dun Superfine dubbing.

Rib: The pheasant tail fibres are ribbed with the dubbed Superfine prior to the building of the body.

Thorax: Red fox squirrel guard hair loop spun and picked out for legs. For rough lough conditions I use a palmered olive grizzle hackle over body dubbing instead of the squirrel dubbing. I clip the hackle flat underneath so the fly sits low on the water.

Wing: Light olive dyed gold bull elk or light olive dyed bucktail with some moose body mixed in for dark veins, tied in with one wing vertical and the other horizontal like a lopsided Wulff fly.

This fly can be fished both dead-drift and also with an occasional 'shiver' to create a small ring pattern around the fly. To do this point the rod at the fly and wiggle the tip side to side until the fly just moves, creating the little rings you see coming from a natural fly struggling in the surface film. Getting the 'shiver' right takes a little practice but the time spent will be well worth it in increased results. Fish react to movement. It is a feeding trigger.

Make base of 20 turns. Tie in wing at centre of base and take thread to bend then forward to hook point.

Tie in tail and take thread to bend.

Wind tail butts to bend and tie in. Dub thread. Rib herl then make body almost to wing base.

Lift wing up and separate into two bunches. set in place with wedge of thread.

Split wing into two and set one horizontal and the other vertical.

Loop spin dubbing and wind the thorax. Neat head. Whip finish.

ACTIVE MAYFLY SPINNER

Normally used later in the afternoon when the females start to come back to the water for egg laying. Initially they simply dip down quickly and are away again almost immediately but eventually they start to rest briefly between short flights as they shed batches of eggs. Fish will target them, launching themselves at the fly as it comes in to drop a bomb of eggs so watch for big, splashy rise forms. A useful pattern to have in your box.

Hook: Standard dry-fly hook size 10 or 12.

Tail: Cock pheasant centre-tail tied at least twice the length of the hook.

Body: Two or three turns of tail-fibre butts ribbed with dubbed thread when forming the rest of the body with light Cahill Superfine dubbing (I used to use white dubbing but have come to prefer the creamy shade).

Hackle: Natural grizzle wound palmer-style over two thirds of the dubbed section of the body.

Wing: Grey-dyed gold bull elk or bucktail with some moose body added to give the venation of the wings.

Head: The wing butts clipped to leave a short bunch over the hook eye.

Fish this fly dead drift for a short distance and then skate it into the lift. Don't leave it on the surface too long.

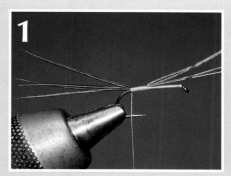

Tie in tail above hook point. Thread to bend.
N.B. Spinner tails are long.

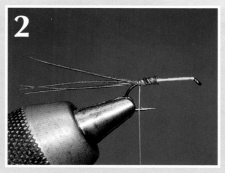

Wind the butts to bend and tie in.

Rib with dubbed thread then form body.
One turn down body.

Tie in hackle and dub back to hook point.

Palmer the hackle down body and rib
through with thread.

Tie in wing. Form head and whip finish. Trim
wing butts.

SKIPPING MAYFLY SPINNER

When fish are lunging after flying spinners, which they often do late on in the hatch, this pattern comes into its own. Essentially it is the same design as the Dancing Dun but using the colours and tail length of the Active Spinner. Use if the Active Spinner is not working.

Hook: Size 10 or 12 dry-fly hook.

Tail: Cock pheasant tail tied twice as long as the body.

Body: Two turns of the tail butts ribbed with light Cahill or white Superfine dubbing then complete the rest of the body with dubbing.

Hackle: Natural grizzle wound in a tight palmer two thirds down the body and a teal or well-marked mallard drake flank feather wound in front.

As with the Dancing Dun this fly fishes well skittered across the nose of an active, jumping fish that is clearly after the egg-laying females.

Tie in tails at point and bind down to bend

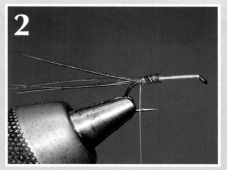

Wind butts down to bend and catch in.

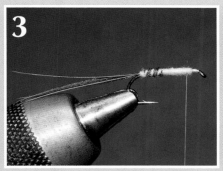

Rib with dubbed thread then form body.

Catch in hackle and dub back down to hook point.

Palmer the hackle tightly and rib thread forward to front.

Strip one side of teal, catch in by tip and wind. Whip finish.

ONE-UP MAYFLY SPINNER

This pattern was born out of my observation of mayflies laying eggs on the River Lathkill in Derbyshire. As the female regularly dips to lay her eggs she eventually becomes exhausted, often ending trapped in the surface film with one wing in the film and the other waving in the air. This pattern is my go-to fly once the fish are on spinners and I seldom use a fully spent fly for the mayfly.

Hook:	Size 10 or 12 standard dry-fly hook such as Kamasan B400, TMC100 or Fulling Mill All Purpose Dry.
Tail:	Cock pheasant tail tied long – at least twice as long as the hook.
Body:	Two turns of the tail butts ribbed with dubbed thread followed by light Cahill Superfine dubbing. Originally I used white rabbit then white Superfine but prefer the light Cahill.
Thorax:	Grey squirrel guard hair or grizzle hackle wound palmer-style over the same dubbing as the body. If using hackle, clip it flat tight underneath.
Wing:	Mixed grey dyed gold elk or bucktail mixed with a few fibres of moose body. The wing is separated like a Wulff wing but set so that one is vertical and the other horizontal.

The fly fishes well when twitched slightly at intervals – point the rod at the fly and wiggle it sideways, NOT up and down, until the fly just shivers on the surface. This takes a bit of practice but can really pull a fish onto a fly. N.B. This is also a good trick when fishing dry daddies, large caddis pattern and dry mayflies which are all large, strong flies.

Make base of 20 turns. Tie in wing at centre of base. Take thread to bend then forward to hook point.

Tie in tail and take thread to bend. N.B.: Tails on spinners are long.

Wind tail butts to bend and tie in. Dub thread. Rib herl and make body almost to wing base.

Lift wing up and set in place with wedge of thread.

Split wing into two and set one horizontal and the other vertical.

Loop spin dubbing and wind the thorax. Form neat head. Whip finish.

TURKEY QUILL SPINNER

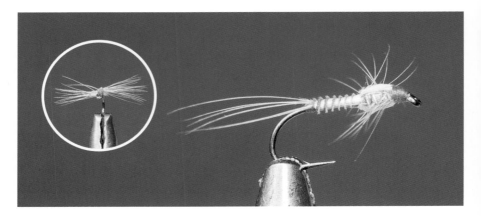

For a long time I used conventional patterns for my spinners but was never really happy with them, partly because of the way the hackle made them sit high off the water. I was looking for a quill type body and simple wings and needed the fly to sit flat on the film. I use a single herl from the long side of a turkey biot quill for the body of these. It is slimmer than the normal dubbing or stripped hackle stems used on other patterns and I find stripped peacock herl too dark.

Hook: Standard dry-fly hook such as Kamasan B400, TMC 100 or TMC103BL size 12 to 20.

Tail: Four to six long cock hackle fibres in light or medium dun – twice the length of the hook. Separate into two bunches.

Body: Turkey primary herl. I use hot orange, yellow, rusty spinner and light Cahill and match the thread as appropriate.

Thorax: Superfine dubbing.

Wings: Cock hackle in light or medium dun or light ginger. Tie as three open turns over the thorax and then spread out sideways so the thorax cover and base can be pulled forward, setting the hackle fibres in the spent position.

Wing case: Two turkey primary herls to match colour of the natural. One pulled from back to front over the top and the other pulled underneath in the same way to set the hackle in the spent position.

Fish this fly dead-drift when you see upwing spinners going to the surface to lay eggs. Seek out stretches where the current has been concentrated by in-water obstructions or on the outside of bends where there is a concentration of drifting food.

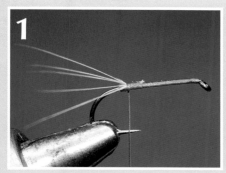

Take thread to bend. Build small 'hump'. take thread forward several turns. Tie in tail fibres. Bind down to bend.

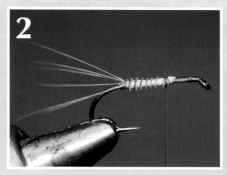

Use thread 'hump' to split tails into two bunches. Tie in quill by tip. Varnish thread and wind body over wet varnish.

Tie in two turkey quills, one on top the other underneath. Take thread forward.

Tie in hackle and then form thorax with dubbed thread back to body.

Make three open turns of hackle. Wind thread forward through hackle.

Pull hackle fibres to sides. Pull quills over on top and bottom. Tie off and whip finish.

UPWINGED FLIES – Fly box suggestions for those purchasing their flies

Below are just a few from many patterns available from good tackle shops and fly-tyers.

Nymphs – size 14 to 18 both weighted and un-weighted.
Sawyer's Pheasant Tail.
Sawyer's Grey Goose.
Pheasant Tail Nymph – natural and dyed olive.
Gold Ribbed Hare's Ear – natural and olive.
Red Fox Squirrel Nymph.
Bead-head versions of the above for extra weight.
Emergers – size 14 to 20.
Klinkhammer – in yellow, light olive, medium olive, grey and tan.
Loop-wing emergers in similar colours.
Dry Flies – size 14 to 20.
F Fly in yellow, olive, grey, and tan.
Adams.
Blue Winged Olive.
Pale Watery or Pale Morning Dun.
Gold Ribbed Hare's Ear.
Spinners – size 14 to 20.
Lunn's Particular.
Sherry Spinner.
Any Hot Orange Spinner.
Apricot Spinner.
Rusty Spinner.
Mayflies – size 10 to 12.
Walker's Mayfly Nymph.
Any Hair or CDC Wing Mayfly Dun – avoid fan wings which 'spin' when casting.
Any Hair or CDC Spent Mayfly.

Sedges or Caddis Flies

Caddis? Sedge? What's in a name? They are one and the same. I grew up with them being called sedge flies – see Halford's Little Red Sedge or the Great Red Sedge (Murrough) – but, more recently, they have become commonly known as caddis flies. I use both terms here. The adult sedge fly is available to the trout from around the end of April in the UK, except for the grannom, which hatches over a very short period in early April. Their larvae however are available all year round, on or near the bottom of the river or lake, and a simple explanation of their life cycle is needed.

Starting from an egg which is laid in an appropriate place, according to the needs of the particular species, the larva hatches out. There are two kinds of larvae that can be easily be imitated. The first are known as case-making larvae and the second as non-case-making larvae. In the case-making forms the grub builds itself a case by spinning a silk-like substance and sticking bits of debris like grains of sand, pebbles, and pieces of weed or sticks together to form a tube into which the body is tucked. As the grub gets bigger so the case needs to be bigger. Once cased, the grub will go about the business of growing, trundling along with the case protecting the soft juicy body whilst it is feeding. One or two case-makers actually build static igloo-like structures rather than the more mobile homes and pop out to feed or intercept passing food items in the current. Caddis cases are very species-specific. Trout will take these mobile grubs, case and all, anywhere they can find them and it is not unusual to find all sorts of mineral debris in

Cased caddis larva using a mix of vegetation and small gravel grains for their cases. Others will use only grains of sand and gravel and others small sticks

Non-cased caddis larva. Note the pair of strong hooks at the rear for holding on tight in fast water. Also see the pale creamy gills showing underneath

the stomach contents of trout feeding in this way.

The non-case-making forms are free-living grubs, most of which live among the gravel, weed and moss including some that build nets to catch their food. Although not wanting this to be a scientific work in any way, it is useful to know the names of a couple of the free-living caddis, namely *Hydropsyche* and *Rhyacophila*, because both are commonly used in modern flyfishing and fly-dressing books and articles. Both types are river flies and important food items.

Once the larva is fully grown it goes into a pupal state before hatching into an adult. At this stage the case-makers fix their cases onto the rocks or weed beds or even rely on the weight of the case, according to their needs, and seal up the entrance. They then go through a metamorphosis rather like a butterfly and change into the adult form. The non-case-making forms build themselves a

Caddis pupal 'Igloos' on rocks in the Derbyshire Derwent. Wade carefully.

little igloo-like structure out of sand and/or gravel and pupate inside. These can easily be seen on the rocks in clear streams. Once the metamorphosis is complete the pupa leaves the case and makes its way to the surface where it hatches into an adult in much the same way as the upwinged flies do.

Once hatched they fly, or in the case of some of the larger species, scuttle along the surface to the bank, creating quite a wake, and then rest up in the trees and bankside vegetation. Unlike upwings, the sedges have rudimentary mouth parts and can take on some sustenance so they have a much longer adult life than the very limited one of the upwings. They are also quite a lot bulkier than upwings, and are easy to recognise, particularly in flight, although some people do mistake them for moths. This confusion can easily be cleared up with a quick look at one at rest. A moth rests with its wings either flat and open, or flat and closed, whereas the sedge rests with its wings set pent, like a pitched roof. They also have straight antennae which are often very long (as in the aptly

Grousewing showing the long, ringed antennae and the very red eyes. Note the long low profile of this species

named longhorn group that includes the grousewing and various silverhorns), rather than the feathery appendages of the moth.

The males use a display flight to attract females and can be seen doing this near the water's edge or over some nearby bush or rush bed. Their display flight is different to the upwings in that the sedges have a more horizontal, side to side movement along with a small vertical, up and down movement. When seen in large numbers at a distance they can resemble a wisp of smoke drifting horizontally back and forth parallel to the ground or over the water. The females are attracted to these swarms and join

them when ready to mate. The males grab the females and the joined pairs usually move into the vegetation to complete the process. Some of the larger sedges seem to find partners in other ways as I have never seen them in large clouds like the smaller species, but then, they do not seem as prolific as, say, the longhorn sedges, so their habits are not as obvious, or it may be that they are more nocturnal in their habits. Suffice it to say that they do get together, usually in the late evening, for I have seen them mating on my boat when fishing into the darkness on the Irish loughs for the big trout that are attracted to them.

Cinnamon sedge – note the shorter antennae and higher profile wing margins

Murrough or great red sedge on my thumb. This fly has to be at least 40mm in length including antennae.

Egg-laying requirements again dictate how the sedge behaves. For instance some river species search out shallows, where they wait until dusk prior to depositing their eggs after swimming or crawling down under the water. Fish will congregate here to feed on them underwater. I was first introduced to this in France back in the late 1990s and it was a revelation. After a hot fishless day I was taken to a small weir in shallow water just on dark and given instructions to tie on my biggest sedge pattern. I was told to cast it into the shallows just downstream of square and to fish it across and down. As the fly came across the stream it reached a point where the current pulled it under. Within seconds I had a hearty take from a decent trout. This was followed in quick succession by a couple of grayling and another trout before the guide called a halt as it was 10.30 and time to stop – night fishing was not allowed here and the bailiffs (the gendarmerie) all carried guns.

Underside of murrough showing the dark body with pronounced segmentation also seen in the pupa

In common with upwings, other sedges will simply fly around dropping 'bombs' of eggs here and there before dying. The dead and dying corpses are taken by trout and grayling as they drift downstream in rivers and the best feeding lies are much

Mating sedges on the surface. A good mouthful!

the same as for spent spinner feeders. On lakes the dying flies are often concentrated in the wind lanes on breezy days but it is possible to get to know areas favoured by different sedges even on the largest waters. Local knowledge is a great asset on somewhere like Lough Corrib where certain bays are well known for the quality of their sedge fishing because of their depth, weed forms and other features. If a bay is known for its large hatches of a fly then it is almost certain to be a bay favoured by the adults returning to lay eggs. By using this knowledge one can often be in the right place at the right time.

STICK FLY

This is a fly that has done well for me for over forty years on stillwaters and is an imitation of the case-making caddis crawling around on the bottom. Fished either as a single fly in small lakes, or as a point fly on larger reservoirs, I use it to search the water if there is no obvious feeding activity. It also works well on rivers but I have another specialist pattern for the river these days.

Hook: Size 10 or 12 heavy wire B175 or similar or long shank nymph hook. Have some unweighted for sunk line work and others leaded to different weights for floating line work, depending on the depth of the water.

Body: Three to five strands of peacock herl, or dubbed squirrel, rabbit or hare body fur either loop-spun and trimmed, or simply dubbed fairly roughly to give a range of colours and textures – caddis cases come in many different forms and a little root around among the stones will often show which ones are present where you fish. I have even seen a mix of deer hair and chopped up cock pheasant tail used to create a spiky case.

Thorax: Chartreuse, cream or amber thread, floss, ultra chenille or wool making a small neat collar suggesting the body of the larva peeping out of the front of the case.

Hackle: Natural black hen or brown partridge hackle – a maximum of two turns.

Head: Black or brown thread built up and varnished.

I fish this dead-drift on rivers and with a slow figure-of-eight retrieve on still waters. It is a good searching pattern for grayling in the winter and for trout in lakes during the early part of the season, before there are large hatches of other flies, and fish are working the bottom layers. This being said, it works at any time on bottom-feeding fish.

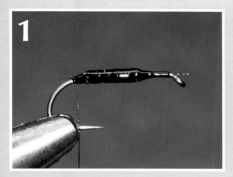

Weight the hook with lead wire. Cover lead with thread and varnish

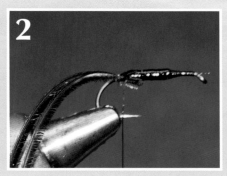

Tie in peacock herl and take thread forward.

Twist herl clockwise round thread and form body.

Tie in chenille and form thorax.

Tie in hackle by tip and make two turns.

Make neat but large head. Whip finish and varnish well for a shiny head.

HEAD DOWN CADDIS LARVA

My river Stick Fly pattern inspired by the Peeping Caddis but with the weight placed at the hook bend rather than the eye. To achieve this I devised the 'bead on a loop' tying. When I weight these I tie the lead wire in layers on the top of the hook so that the fly fishes point uppermost. Before I came up with this pattern I used a standard Stick Fly with a lot of success, especially for grayling. Fish this fly upstream, dead drift to suggest a dislodged caddis trying to get back to the safety of the river bed. Very good in hatch and weir pools where there are deep back eddies.

Hook: Size 10 or 12 wet fly hook or 2x nymph hook. The main weight here is in the tungsten or brass bead but, for deep, fast runs it pays to have some weighted with lead as well.

Head: Tied in first to sit over the bend of the hook. Black, copper or brown bead threaded onto a short length of micro chenille or Antron yarn in chartreuse, cream or amber. This chenille or yarn is then tied in so that the bead is set over the bend of the hook showing a small hotspot of colour.

Hackle: A few fibres of natural black hen or brown partridge hackle tied in at the bend rather like a tail. Splay the fibres as you tie them in so they sit out on either side of the head.

Body: Peacock herl or loop-spun furs like hare, rabbit or squirrel.

Fish this fly upstream, dead-drift, to suggest a dislodged caddis trying to get back to the safety of the river bed. Very good in hatch- and weir-pools where there are deep back-eddies.

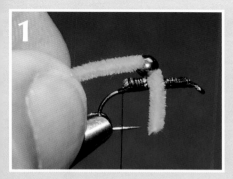

Lead hook with layers of flat lead. Varnish. Thread bead on chenille.

Tie looped chenille and bead at the bend like a tail.

Tie in a small bunch of hackle fibres each side.

Loop spin the chosen body material (rabbit in this case) and form the body. Whip finish.

Trim close to give a sandy look. (Coarser materials give heavier look).

With the bead at the tail and layers of lead on the back of the hook the fly should fish head down.

NON CASED CADDIS

This is my take on the Czech nymph. The rivers in Derbyshire are full of caseless caddis and the fish love them. Most are dark browns and olives and I have also seen some that are quite orangey. There is also the green Rhyacophila larva that lives in the moss and weed beds.

Hook: Size 10 or 12 nymph hook. Some need to be leaded with up to two layers of lead wire to get down deep quickly but have some unleaded for fishing the shallow runs as well – make sure you have a range of weights.

Tail: Two butts of pheasant tail fibres trimmed short. You can leave the quill curl on if you like as the naturals have 2 curved claws at the rear for holding themselves in position in the strong currents where they live.

Back: Brown Thin Skin or Orange Bustard or Oak Mottled Thin Skin or similar – use olive or clear for the green version. This is pulled over after the body has been dubbed then ribbed tightly to create segments.

Body: Natural rabbit or squirrel dubbing dyed shades of olive and tied fairly slim but taken round the bend to give a little curve to the fly. Pick out lightly underneath. For the green version use caddis green or light olive dubbing and pick out on the sides instead of underneath.

Rib: Copper wire.

Thorax: As for body but slightly built up.

Legs: Partridge back feather tied in by the butt before the thorax is dubbed and then pulled over and tied at the front. Pinch the off fibres fairly short as the legs are not very long at this stage.

Thorax: The back material pulled over and tied off at the front.

Fish this dead-drift in the streams. It can work well at almost any time as fish may feed hard near the bottom at almost any time of the year.

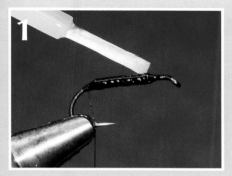

Wind lead wire from the bend to the thorax area. Cover with thread and varnish

Tie in tails with 3/4 turns round bend.

Catch in back material and rib.

Dub the body to thorax area.

Pull back over and rib. Catch in partridge feather. Dub Thorax.

Pull partridge feather forward. Pull back over and tie off. Whip finish.

CADDIS PUPA

My version of the old favourite, Bell's Amber Nymph, which I have been using virtually unchanged since the late 1960s.

Hook: Size 10 to 14 for stillwater fishing and down to size 18 for rivers. Have some on dry-fly hooks for surface work as well as others on heavier wire hooks to fish deeper. I do not usually weight this pattern.

Body: Seal's fur taken just onto the bend to give a curve. I use amber, dark claret or olive with the amber version being my favourite. Other colours will be needed on some waters, so experiment.

Back: Cock pheasant centre tail fibres tied in at the bend and then pulled forward over the body to the thorax point. Use peacock herl for a darker back.

Rib: Gold oval tinsel, stretched pearl tinsel, gold wire, copper wire or other appropriate UTC wire colours wound after the back has been pulled forward over the abdomen.

Thorax: Fiery brown or dark brown seal's fur, or try a darker shade of olive on the olive pattern.

Wing case: Cock pheasant centre tail or 2mm of brown foam for a more buoyant pattern.

Legs/Wings: Picked out seal's fur, or tips of pheasant tail fibres pulled down and back, or two turns of brown partridge feather (stripped one side) pulled down and back.

On stillwaters I fish a team of these a using figure-of-eight retrieve or even static with an occasional draw. On rivers I normally fish them dead-drift with an occasional draw to make them rise in the water but, as in all fishing, experiment until you find the correct combination for the day.

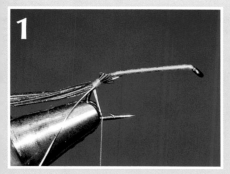

Tie in back material with 3/4 turns round the hook bend. Tie in rib.

Dub the body up to thorax area.

Pull back over and rib.

Tie in wing case material and leave tips out over eye.

Dub thorax. Pull feather tips back and down to form legs.

Bring wing case over. Form head. Whip finish.

LOOP WINGED CADDIS EMERGER

This is my take on the Loop-winged Hopper which can be so good in a sedge hatch.

Hook: Grub hook or York Bend hook size 10 to 16 – one of the very few curved hooks I use because it is necessary to give the fly the right attitude.

Body: Seal's fur (Superfine dubbing in smaller sizes). I use amber (my favourite), claret and olive mostly, but tan and rusty brown are also good.

Rib: Stretched medium pearl Mylar or copper wire in smaller sizes.

Thorax: Seal's fur a shade darker than the body.

Wing: Three CDC feathers looped over the thorax.

Legs: Picked out fibres from thorax. I sometimes add a pair of knotted pheasant tail fibre legs tied in behind the thorax on larger sizes.

For me this is more a stillwater pattern, but it is worth fishing on a river during sedge hatches. Fish dead-drift on rivers and static with the occasional twitch on stillwaters.

Tie in the thread, catch in rib and dub thread.

Form the body.

Wind rib forward.

Catch in the CDC feathers.

Dub thread and form thorax.

Pull CDC over to complete loop. Whip finish.

DADE CADDIS

I was given this pattern back in the 1970s and keep coming back to it as the best overall design I have found. It is named for Reg Dade, one-time keeper on the Bossington water on the Test. I have varied the original slightly over the years to suit a range of caddis colours.

Hook: Size 10 to 16 dry-fly hook or a 2x long shank nymph hook sizes 10 and 12 for the Murrough and Green Peter.

Body: Superfine dubbing in caddis green, cinnamon caddis, tan, rusty brown, grey, hare's ear and any other that suits the natural.

Wing: Originally grey squirrel tail but I also use fox squirrel, brown bucktail and even moose body. This is tied in by the centre and then folded back on itself to form a 'bullet head'. The wing is then clipped at an angle just longer than the hook.

Hackle: Cock hackle wound over the tied down part of the wing and then clipped flat underneath. Hackle colours to suit the colour tied but usually dun, ginger or red game.

N.B. If you want to skate this fly then tie some without trimmed hackles as I find the trimmed ones allow the fly to dive when pulled. This is great at egg-laying time but not during a hatch.

A fly for rivers and stillwaters. Fish this both dead-drift and with movement. A great river pattern to fish at the tail of shallows in the late evening when the sedges are egg laying. Cast across almost square and allow the fly to drift downstream, skating and then diving under as the current catches it. Wait for the hard pulls! On lakes this fly has been successful in all sizes, right down to size 18.

Take thread to bend. Dub thread and form body.

Tie in small bunch of hair by the centre and tie down tightly to the eye.

Pull the forward hair back and bind tightly to complete wing.

Trim wing at an angle. Take thread forward again.

Tie in hackle. Take thread back to wing.

Wind hackle in touching turns and rib through. Whip finish.

SEDGE FLIES - Fly box suggestions for those purchasing their flies

Below are just a few from many patterns available from good tackle shops and fly-tyers.

Nymphs – size 10 to 14.
Stick Fly.
Czech Nymphs – select one or two colours only from a huge range and make sure you have more than one weight.
Peeping Caddis.
Pupae – size 10 to 16.
Amber Nymph – seek out similar flies in other colours, especially olive, claret and fiery brown.
Gold Ribbed Hare's Ear in natural and olive.
Emergers – size 10 to 16.
Hopper – various colours including hare's ear, claret, olive, orange and amber.
CDC Hoppers – as for Hopper.
Dry Sedges – sizes 10 to 16.
Halford's Little Red Sedge.
Cinnamon Sedge.
March Brown.
CDC and Elk.
Elk Hair Caddis – pick a range of colours to include cinnamon, tan, olive and grey.
Green Peter.
Murrough (Murragh).

Stone Flies and Needle Flies

While working on limestone rivers in Derbyshire for many years I saw very little activity by the adults of the larger stoneflies, despite their nymphs being very common, so I am tempted to ignore the adults as being of little real value. However, there are some places in the USA and elsewhere that have huge hatches of large stoneflies (often called salmon flies in the USA) and I have seen them in flight during the day in quite large numbers on rivers in eastern France, so where they do prevail in good numbers they can be important food items.

For me it is the smaller species that are of most interest. The yellow sally, willow fly and needle flies amongst them. The noticeable difference between the stonefly and the needle fly is in the way they fold their wings at rest. The stone fly has wings that sit low and flat over the body and which appear roughly teardrop shaped. The needle fly folds its wings more tightly to the body

A small brown stonefly. Note the shape of the wings at rest

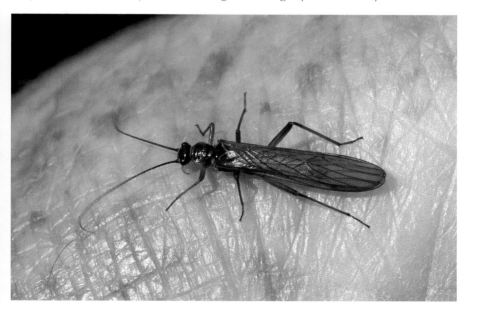

Large stonefly on a post beside the Derbyshire Wye. Almost put my hand on it going over a stile

so that they are pointed and less visible, hence the name. The nymph tends to crawl rather than swim and is a clumsy swimmer at best so, for this reason I do not specifically imitate the nymph although there are numerous stonefly nymph patterns available. This group of flies has no pupal stage and, when fully developed, the nymph crawls out onto rocks and other emergent objects to hatch rather than hatching on the water surface. This being said I

A needle fly showing the more tightly rolled pointed wing at rest

do use imitations of the adult with quite some success when I see them about in large numbers.

When egg laying, these smaller stoneflies are of interest to the fish as they dip down to the surface depositing 'bombs' of eggs. Fish actively seek them out and I have actually caught fish that were specialising in catching the flies in the act of dipping to lay eggs. I am sure the fish see them coming in the air and target them deliberately, in much the same way as they do with larger mayflies and sedge coming in to lay eggs. Fish feeding this way seem to launch themselves at the flies, often clearing the water in the process. Whilst most stoneflies are river species some are also found in the richer lakes, Scottish lochs and Irish loughs, although I have never heard of anyone imitating them on stillwaters. That is not to say that, where they are found, it would not go amiss to try a suitable imitation.

Early autumn on the Derbyshire Derwent, a time when small stone and needle fly imitations work well for both trout and grayling

BIOT WING STONE FLY

When the little yellow sally is about from the end of May onwards, followed by the willow fly and needle flies of late summer and autumn, there are times, especially in the middle of the day, when these get on to the water. Originally tied as a Wonderwing pattern I changed to the Biot-wing to represent the scaly wing of these flies. Both styles work well.

Hook: Size 12 to 16 dry-fly hook.

Body: Superfine dubbing. I use pale morning dun for the yellow sally and Adams grey and dark tan for the darker flies. Add a couple of turns of yellow at the tail of the sally and light orange on the other two if you wish.

Hackle: Light olive or light ginger for the yellow sally and ginger or dark dun for the others. This is wound palmer-style over the front half of the body then clipped top and bottom so that the fly sits very low on the water.

Wing: Turkey biot tied down flat over the hook – see illustration. I use olive or grey for the yellow sally and brown for the darker patterns. The stone fly wings are rounded at the ends and set flat at rest while the needle flies have tightly rolled wings that appear pointed so, for the latter; I tie the biot in so the narrow end is showing.

Fish dead-drift. This is a good trout pattern for me on rivers, especially on hot summer days when the fish seem to take them around midday. Later in the year they work well for grayling right into November.

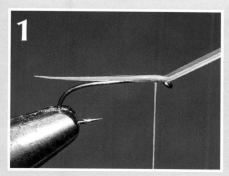

Make a base of thread then tie in turkey biot concave side up

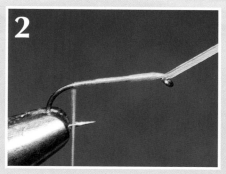

Tie down to bend.

Form the dubbed body to thorax area.

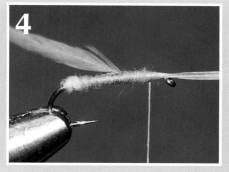

Catch in hackle and then dub the thorax area as far as the eye.

Wind hackle in open turns and rib back through it. Trim out top hackle fibres.

Pull biot back over and tie down behind thorax. Whip finish. Trim out lower hackles.

EGG-LAYING STONE FLY

I have watched trout target these flies as they bomb down and deposit their balls of eggs on the surface. The fly only touches down momentarily but the fish seem to see them coming and intercept them as they hit the surface, often coming very fast at the fly. This is really a modernised version of the old West Country favourite of my youth, the Half Stone.

Hook: Size 12 to 14 dry-fly hook.

Eggs: Ball of Superfine dubbing in pale yellow or light Cahill.

Body: Superfine dubbing. I use pale morning dun for the yellow sally and Adams grey, rusty brown and dark tan for the darker flies.

Hackle: Light dun for the yellow sally and medium or dark dun for the darker flies. This is wound palmer-style over the front two thirds of the fly.

Fish this at any time of the day when you see the stoneflies coming in to lay their eggs. The egg sac is fairly visible on the naturals and you will see them dip down to the surface repeatedly as they fly about, depositing their eggs in little 'bombs.' I have seen fish take these flies on the wing as they come in to lay their eggs.

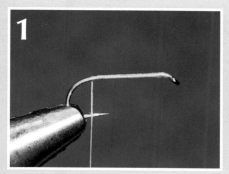

Take thread down to the bend.

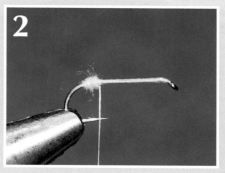

Dub the egg sac.

Dub the rest of the body almost to the eye and take one turn back.

Tie in hackle and dub back down to the hook point.

Palmer the hackle down and tie in.

Rib the thread forward and form the head. Whip finish.

STONE FLIES - Fly box suggestions for those purchasing their flies

Below are just a few from many patterns available from good tackle shops and fly-tyers.

Nymphs – size 10 to 16.
Montana Nymph
yellow or orange thorax versions.
Long shank Pheasant Tail.
Long shank Gold Ribbed Hare's Ear.
Dry Stoneflies – size 12 to 16.
Half Stone.
Honey Dun Half Stone.
Double Badger.
Stimulator – size 12 to 16 but larger sizes if large stoneflies are present on your water.

Buzzers or Chironomids

Probably the single most important food source in stillwaters of all kinds, the life cycle of this group of flies is not fully understood by many fishermen. From the egg comes a larva, often called a bloodworm. This is a slim worm-like grub that comes in a range of colours, red, olive, and orange to name but a few, and can be found in the bottom detritus of virtually any water, however big or small. Here it remains until it is ready to change into a pupa when it retreats into a burrow and from there goes into metamorphosis. Occasionally in the high summer bloodworm migrate to the top for a time, usually late in the day only to drop back again some time later. When this happens excellent fishing can be had with a bloodworm pattern fished on the drop.

A grey boy pupa ejected by a Corrib trout

When it is ready to hatch, the pupa rises up to the surface where it hangs for a short time before breaking through the surface tension and splitting down the back of the thorax, allowing the adult fly to emerge onto the surface. During the ascent from the deeps the pupa pumps blood into the wings and legs to energise them. This blood causes the wings to glow orange in many, but not all, species and it is not uncommon to see a newly hatched fly change from bright orange to black or olive as it dries and hardens off before flight. For this reason orange is prevalent in the wing cases of many pupal imitations. Once hatched, the flies fly or, in some cases scuttle, along the surface, and take refuge in the trees and bushes along the banks until it is time to breed.

The males of most species create a dancing swarm to attract the females. These swarms are often heard before they are seen as the males make a high pitched buzzing noise as they swarm which can be heard many yards away, hence the name buzzer, although both sexes make a high pitched buzzing noise in flight. The females fly up into the swarm and, once mated, will make for

Male buzzer – note the slim build and the feathery antennae

water where they will begin egg-laying. This may be immediately or after a brief resting period. The females often carry the first batch of eggs already extruded as they head for the water and, as with some upwings, they fly with their bodies vertical and the very tail end hooked forward like an upside down question mark. Initially they skim about on the surface as they lay their eggs until they become exhausted and finally lay on the surface, making shivering movements as they slowly die. Some other evening hatching buzzers form a mating frenzy on the water, appearing as a large ball or cluster of mixed adults and the fish can become obsessed with them, especially on Irish loughs like Corrib where anglers will stay out all night waiting for the 'fly to ball'. One or two species can be seen mating on the water during the day. As soon as the females hatch the males, which are hawking backwards and forwards, skim the surface while searching for the hatching females. They pounce on them and mate with them before they have even dried their wings. I have filmed Grey Boy buzzers doing just that.

Fish will feed on all stages of the buzzers life cycle in a day, starting deep down near the bottom feeding on bloodworm

Female buzzer – note the heavy build and small antennae

Mating pair of grey boy buzzers still on the surface. Note the orange wings and the discarded shuck, sure signs she has only just hatched

and then, as the pupae get active and leave their burrows, gradually working up through the water column during the day, the fish follow them up, until the flies hatch, feeding hard on every stage. They will then wait until the egg-laying starts and target them when they come back to the water again to lay eggs.

In the early season particularly, when buzzer hatches are at their biggest, anglers that know this are constantly changing patterns, weights of fly and even line types throughout the day to keep up with the fish as they change depth to stay with the hatching flies. On other days, of course, the fish feed hard on only one stage all day and if this is down deep then they can be hard to find as there are no visible signs of feeding. Fishing at the right depth is absolutely critical on these days.

A female egg-laying buzzer. She is not yet fully spent so not flat on the surface.

BLOODWORM

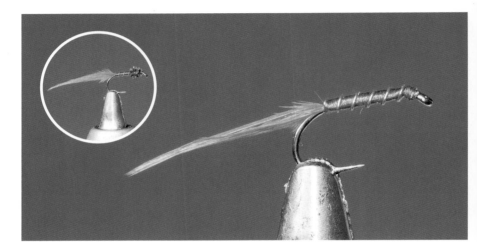

I first tied this pattern way back in 1970 with some success. It is not a fly I use much these days but, for me at least, it is far more successful than the modern rubber band versions. Very much a lake pattern for me but I have found many bloodworms in kick samples taken on the Derbyshire rivers, so well worth a try on streams.

Hook: Size 10 or 12 short shank wet fly hook like the B160.

Head: For weighted flies only, add a small 2mm red tungsten bead before dressing the fly.

Tail: Red marabou – the poor quality thinner tips of the feather or soft flue from a dyed red goose shoulder. Also try it in olive and black.

Body: Red floss silk.

Rib: Red wire or none.

Thorax: I tie some with a peacock herl thorax (inset) suggesting a pupa rather than the bloodworm. Both patterns work well.

The fly is no more than an inch long in total with the marabou giving the 'wiggle factor' for both larva and pupa.

Fish deep when seeking fish that are not feeding near the surface, or where they can actually be seen feeding on the bottom. Experiment with depth and be ready for takes 'on the drop.' The first version I used was with the peacock herl thorax and I fished this hanging in the surface film over buzzer feeding fish working the surface layers. I well remember the first fish on this fly, a four-pound brownie from Blagdon way back in the early 70's.

Tie in the marabou tail at the bend.

Tie in the rib and body floss. Take thread forward.

Wind the floss to form a slim body.

Form body and rib almost to eye and whip finish.

For thorax version leave room at head end and catch in peacock herl.

Twist herl clockwise round thread and make thorax. Whip finish.

DEEP BUZZER

My version of the Superglue Buzzer, tied after having had a close look at one wriggling about on a boat seat after catching a fish.

Hook: Size 8 to 14 medium or heavyweight wet fly hook such as B175, B170 or B160.

Body: Tying thread taken just round the bend of the hook – colour choices include black, olive and claret – with either turkey primary herl in black, grey or olive from the non-biot side of the feather wound in touching turns for the large sizes or natural or dyed peacock eye quill on the smaller sizes wound in almost touching turns to show a little thread.

Thorax: Tying thread only slightly built up.

Cheeks: Orange or fiery brown goose biots.

Top of Head: Chartreuse or sunburst yellow goose biot pulled over the top.

Coating: The whole fly is coated with either Sally Hansen Hard As Nails or UV epoxy.

As the name suggests this fly is fished very slowly, or static, deep down where the fish are picking the buzzer pupae off as they leave the bottom of the lake for the surface to hatch. Beware the hard takes that you often get fishing this fly and always be ready for takes on the drop.

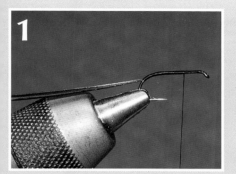

Take thread round bend and catch in the turkey quill. Take thread to thorax position.

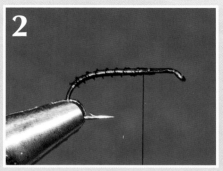

Varnish thread and wind quill in touching turns.

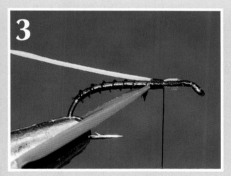

Catch in orange biots under hook and chartreuse biot on top of hook.

Form thorax with smooth layers of thread.

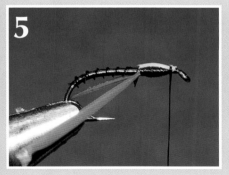

Pull chartreuse biot forward and tie in.

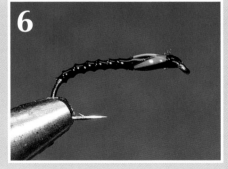

Pull each orange biot up and forward. Tie off. Whip finish and varnish whole fly well.

HERL BUZZER

This is my favourite pattern for fishing high in the water column. I like herl bodies when fishing up in the water as they create a softer look with some translucence when fished near the surface. Thank the late Dick Walker for this one. I have been using this pattern ever since I read his article about it back in the late 1960s and it still keeps on catching.

Hook: Size 10 to 16 dry-fly hook – I prefer straight hooks for my buzzers.

Tail: Tiny tuft of white floss, baby wool, hackle fibre or marabou – and I do mean tiny.

Body: Dyed goose herl in black, red, dark claret, olive or green taken just round the bend of the hook.

Rib: White hackle stem, stripped, or stretched medium pearl Mylar – a modern tweak to the original design.

Thorax: Peacock herl.

Cheeks: Orange goose biots. Originally we did not use the goose biots at all and the flies still worked.

Breathers: As for tail.

Fish this static and greased up in the film or just under when the fish are bulging the surface with their shoulders. It is a good pattern to fish in a team with the Loop-wing Buzzer and Shuttlecock Buzzer.

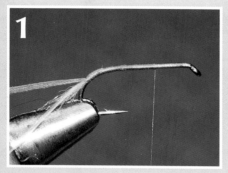

Tie in tail, rib and body herl just round the bend of the hook. Take thread back up hook.

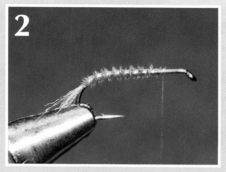

Wind the herl up the hook then wind the rib up on the other spiral.

Tie in a tuft of white poly yarn at the eye.

Catch in two orange biots under the hook.

Tie in 2/3 peacock herls. Twist round thread and form thorax.

Bring biots up and forward. Tie off. Whip finish and trim tufts to length.

SHUTTLECOCK BUZZER EMERGER

Tied to represent that period when the adult is just about to break out of its nymphal shuck by splitting the back of the thorax. When the Loop-wing Emerger is not working this pattern often will – something to do with way they sit in the water, I think, so when fish are feeding in the film I use both on the same leader until I find which they want.

Hook: Size 10 to 16 dry-fly hook.

Tail: Short stub of white floss or hackle fibres.

Body: Dyed peacock quill, goose herl or tying thread in appropriate colours with black, olive and claret being the most common for me.

Rib: Stretched medium pearl Mylar if using goose or thread body.

Thorax: Thread built up just a little.

Shuttlecock: CDC plumes, one orangey red and three natural tied in behind thorax, pulled over tight and tied down in front leaving the tips poking out over the hook eye. In the smaller sizes I reduce to two natural and one orange CDC but I find a size 10 or 12 needs at least four feathers to float the fly in anything more than a light ripple. Use fewer and your fly will keep sinking. I found out the hard way.

Fish this fly dead-drift with the occasional little pull to just twitch the fly, giving it 'life.'

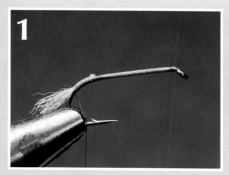

Take thread round bend and tie in tail tuft.

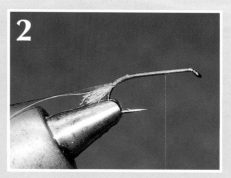

Catch in rib and body herl (if using herl).

Form the body up to the thorax area. Wind rib (counter wind if over herl).

Tie in CDC as a bunch with tips about level with hook bend.

Form thorax with smooth layers of thread.

Pull CDC over and tie down. Whip finish.

LOOP WING BUZZER EMERGER

For years I struggled with the emerging buzzer stage, fishing herl flies greased up in the hope of keeping them in the film. It did work some of the time but the CDC loop-wing has made film fishing really work for me. My use of mallard flank shucks on buzzers goes back to the late 1960s but now CDC has arrived I am very taken with it as a shuck material.

Hook: Size 10 to 16 lightweight grub hook or York bend hook such as Fulling Mill's Living Nymph Hook – one of the very few curved hooks I use because it is necessary to give the fly the right attitude.

Tail: A few fibres of mallard drake flank feather or pale natural CDC as a shuck.

Body: Dyed goose herl, preferred, or dyed peacock eye quill or tying thread in appropriate colours.

Rib: Stretched medium pearl Mylar.

Thorax: Superfine dubbing or peacock herl.

Wing: CDC plumes – one orangey red under two or three natural grey tied in behind the thorax and then pulled over into a loop.

Fish this in exactly the same way as the Shuttlecock version.

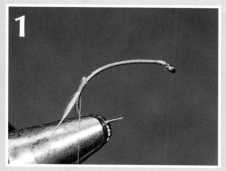

Take thread round bend and tie in tail tuft.

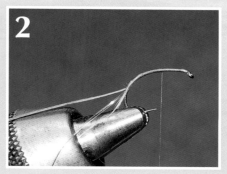

Tie in rib and body herl.

Form body and then rib on the other spiral.

Tie in two natural CDC feathers and one orange Cdec.

Form thorax.

Pull orange CDC over top and then nat. CDC's to mask it. Tie off. Whip finish.

BUZZERS – Fly box suggestions for those purchasing their flies.

Below are just a few from many patterns available from good tackle shops and fly-tyers.

Make sure you have some in each of these colours: black, olive, red and claret and in sizes 10 to 16.

Deep Buzzers.
Superglue Buzzers – there are so many to choose from so be selective but err on the subtle side rather than the gaudy.
Mid-water Buzzers – make a selection from these styles.
Floss body Buzzers.
Herl body Buzzers.
Quill body Buzzers.
Emerger/Dry Buzzers.
Shuttlecock Buzzers.
Klinkhåmer Buzzers.
Hoppers
Shipman's Buzzers.
Palomino Midge.

Terrestrials

Trout are opportunist feeders a lot of the time; especially when natural, waterborne food is scarce and they will readily take a wide range of insects that get blown onto the water. There are quite a few species that appear seasonally on the water, causing frenzied feeding on occasion, as well as some that appear regularly throughout most of the summer.

DADDY LONG LEGS OR CRANE FLY

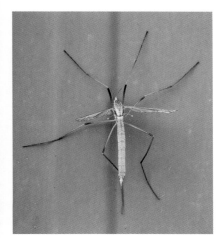

Female daddy long legs

Crane flies are particularly abundant in May, August and September when the fish will feed avidly on them in both rivers and lakes. This is a substantial mouthful for a fish and well worth imitating. Warm, damp days seem to favour this fly and, with an offshore wind blowing, especially near field systems, you can have some great dry-fly fishing, or even dapping, with an artificial.

HAWTHORN FLY

This is a fairly large black fly with long trailing back legs that flies at the end of April or early May when the hawthorn bush comes into leaf. The males are to be seen hovering near bushes in the heat of the day, looking for all the world like a mini black helicopter. They are jet black, have a pronounced thorax, slim abdomen and clear, sparkling wings. The females are also black but much more heavily built, usually a hook size larger and have darker wings. Hawthorns fall on the water regularly and are a seasonal feast for trout wherever they fall. I have noticed that at times mating pairs fall into the water from the bushes and, if this is happening in any numbers, I have seen fish become fixated on the joined pairs only.

Mating hawthorns – female is the large one

HEATHER FLY OR BIBIO

Related to the hawthorn fly this one hatches towards the end of July and into August when the heather starts to bloom. Similar in every way to the hawthorn the only obvious difference is in the long back legs which are reddish-brown. The trout like them every bit as much as they do the hawthorn flies when they are on the water. Again, the body and wing difference between male and female is the same as for the hawthorn.

BLACK GNAT

Mating black gnats – the female is the darker one

Another, much smaller relation of the hawthorn fly, this can be found on the wing from April onwards and is a favourite of the fish when it is on the water in any numbers. The wing colour difference is shown clearly in the picture and, as with many apparently clear wings, there is a sheen on them rather like oil on water. It is fair to point out here that, because there are so many small black terrestrial flies around in the summer, a black gnat imitation is a must in any fly fisherman's box, for use even when the true black gnat is not actually on the water.

N.B. I have used the term bibio for the heather fly only, although these last three flies are actually all members of the genus, Bibio. This is because the name bibio has been used specifically for the heather fly and its imitation for many decades, particularly in Scotland and Ireland.

FLYING ANTS

High summer in late July and early August will sometimes see huge falls of flying ants on the water. When this happens the general advice is that, unless you have a good imitation, go home and come back another day as trout seem to have a real taste for these small creatures and become fixated on them. It takes a good imitation to fool them into taking. I seldom carry one myself but have been known to rue the day when a fall happens.

Black ant about to fly over Corrib

BEETLES

From time to time during the summer months land beetles and weevils get blown onto the water in large numbers and they form an important part of the terrestrial insect part of the fish's diet. Some, like the Coch-y-Bonddu (Bracken Beetle), are historically well known and can be found on lakes and rivers during early Summer when they get blown off the heath land. If they do find their way onto your water, chances are the fish will glut on them to the exclusion of everything else. Other brightly coloured beetles likely to find their way onto the water are the ladybird, soldier and sailor beetles, and even shield bugs that frequent the meadows and bushes along the water's edge.

As well as these there are numerous small beetles, usually black, found on the trees overhanging the water and they frequently drop into the river where they are eaten with relish. They seem particularly popular with the trout on hot summer days when other flies are not hatching and having an imitation in your box can mean the difference between a very slow day and a good day. Fish them in shady spots where trees or other vegetation overhang the water, in the eddies formed below mature alder trees or where

Clockwise from top left: Shield Bug, ladybird, soldier beetle and the lesser known sailor beetle, all taken by trout. Could the success of the Bibio pattern be partly down to the sailor beetle and the Soldier Palmer pattern be down to the soldier beetle I wonder?

an undercut bank gives some shade, normally on the outside of a river bend. On lakes they can be blown onto the water from the trees on the upwind banks and drift across to where the trout are waiting.

CATERPILLARS

There are numerous small caterpillars to be found on the alder, willow and other trees ranged along the banks of streams and rivers as well as many lakes, some of which drop down on a silk thread prior to pupating. These small caterpillars get knocked and/or blown into the water and are much loved by fish. Trout especially will congregate 'line astern' just downstream of overhanging trees ready to pick up the fallen caterpillars as they drop. The ones I have seen are either pale chartreuse green or a grey/olive brown. At times it can be useful to have a pattern in the box. I do not have my own pattern but if you want a pattern then look no further than the Inch Worm pattern tied with fine Ultra Chenille, deer hair or foam. The name says it all. They are literally an inch long, if that.

DADDY LONG LEGS

I do not like deer hair or foam for extended bodies. They look great but are very stiff and I believe they can result in many missed takes. I took the Palamino Midge body idea and came up with this pattern which is working well for me.

Hook: Size 10 or 12 short shank hook such as B160 or a B100 grub hook.

Body: Golden brown or tan Ultra Chenille (small size) with the end lightly singed to taper it. Try not to burn it! I am not a fan of detached bodies, especially foam ones, but the Ultra Chenille collapses better than any deer hair or foam when a fish takes.

Legs: Knotted cock pheasant tail fibres.

Thorax: Two turns of body material to give a little bulk behind the wings.

Hackle: Light ginger or light dun to enhance the wing and sit the fly up at an angle. I also tie some without any hackle for when the flies are laying in the surface film drowning.

Wings: Brown bucktail tied nearly spent.

Fish this in both rivers and lakes whenever there is a fall of 'daddies' or at any time in late May and from August onwards when they are likely to be around. On large loughs in Ireland fish will often take them just because they are there, whether there is a hatch going on or not. For this reason it is a good searching dry fly late in the season.

Make a base of about 20 turns of thread.

Tie in the bucktail wing and cover the butts.

Tie in a length of chenille (tapered with lighter).

Take thread to front of wing and separate into two wings almost spent. Take thread back behind wings.

Make 2 turns of chenille and tie off. Tie in three knotted legs each side. Thread to front of wings.

Tie in hackle taking thread to body. Wind hackle. Rib through and tie off. Whip finish.

MATING HAWTHORNS

When mating, the hawthorns sometimes get blown into the water on windy days and I have found that if this happens fish can become pre-occupied with the mating pairs rather than the single fly. I first tied this pattern up in the late 70s when working on the Hampshire Avon, after observing some 'uncatchable' trout feeding on hawthorns below a small bush on a carrier. It took at least an hour to work out that the fish were feeding selectively on mated pairs only. I had already had success with Tom Ivens' Fuzzy Wuzzy dry flies on local stillwaters and took the initial idea from there to develop this fly. I also tie a version with reddish legs for later in the season when the Heather Fly is about. The only difference is that the legs are either reddish brown turkey primary herl or cock pheasant tail.

Hook: Size 10 or 12 2X long dry-fly hook like the TMC 5212.

Rear Hackle: Black cock wound at the bend and clipped underneath.

Body: Rear half black tying thread. Front half black Superfine dubbing or ostrich herl.

Legs: Knotted black turkey primary herl – just one set tied in at the front.

Front Hackle: Black cock clipped underneath.

Fish as any dry fly but do not be afraid to give it a bit of movement as the naturals are usually struggling in the surface film.

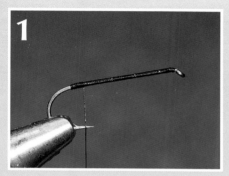

Take thread down hook to bend then eight turns forwards.

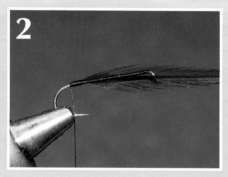

Catch in hackle and bind stem down to bend.

Wind hackle to bend. Rib through it and take thread to mid shank in touching turns.

Dub thread (or catch in ostrich herl) and form body.

Knot two turkey quills and tie in facing backwards. Thread to front of hook.

Tie in hackle. Dub thread to body. Wind hackle. Rib thread through and whip finish. Trim wide V in each hackle.

BIOT WING BLACK GNAT

This pattern is not a million miles away from the ancient Pike Scale Black Gnat of the late 1800s. The male black gnat is a much slimmer fly than the female so note the two dressings included here.

Hook: Size 16 to 20 dry-fly hook.

MALE (inset) showing clipped hackle to give a low profile.

Body: Rear half black tying thread. Front half black Superfine dubbing.

Wing: White turkey biot.

Hackle: Black cock hackle tied palmer over the front half of the body then trimmed top and bottom so that the fly sits low.

FEMALE – dressed in the same style but fatter.

Body: Black Superfine dubbing right through giving more bulk.

Wing: Black or dark grey turkey biot.

Hackle: Black cock hackle tied palmer over the front half of the body then trimmed top and bottom so that the fly sits low.

Fish this fly dead-drift, in the surface-film rather than on it. Good during the day when there is little sign of other hatches, or when your olive patterns have been ignored.

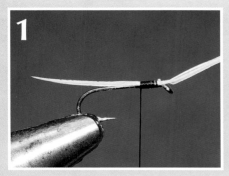

Make a base of thread and tie in the turkey biot at the eye, concave side up.

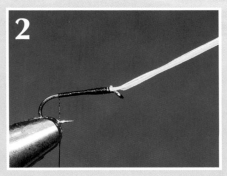

Take the thread to the bend. For the female dub thread here. For the male take the thread half way back up hook then dub.

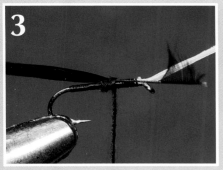

Form the body to 3/4 mark then catch in hackle.

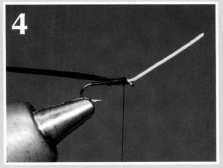

Complete the dubbed body to the eye.

Wind hackle forward and rib thread back through to rear of thorax. Trim hackle off top.

Pull turkey biot back and tie off. Whip finish. Trim wing to length and trim out wide V in lower hackle fibres.

DARK TERRESTRIAL

I first dressed this fly for the River Lathkill back in the late 1980s to tackle some high summer, mid-day feeding fish taking smallish black terrestrials when there was no hatch of fly at all. Having no Black Gnats with me and in some desperation, as I was guiding one of the Duke's guests, I selected from his box a very battered size 14 Black and Peacock Spider with bits of peacock herl sticking out of the body. Although it worked like a charm it was a little large so I went home and set to work on a fine-tuned version for the next day. This fly was the result and it has gone on working ever since.

Hook: Size 16 to 24 dry-fly hook. Tied in sizes 12 and 14 it will do for the hawthorn hatch.

Body: Rear half black thread tied slim. Front half two strands of peacock herl.

Wings: The tips of the body herl pointing back over the hook bend and clipped.

Hackle: Natural black. I also use dark dun or grizzle as variations. The hackle is clipped top and bottom so the fly sits very low on the water.

Fish this fly as you would the Black Gnat. I find it works well on hot summer days when fish can be found in shady spots feeding on 'nothing in particular.'

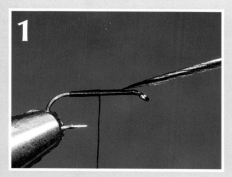

Take eight turns of thread from eye. Tie in hackle. Take thread down to bend.

Form thread body half way up hook.

Tie in two thin peacock herls with tips out over bend.

Wind the butts forward to hackle and back again. Tie in.

Wind the hackle in open turns down the hook to the thread and tie in.

Rib thread through hackle. Whip finish. Trim hackle off top and bottom and trim wings to length.

FOAM BEETLE

This is not really my pattern as it is pretty universal but it works on hot days in the middle of the summer, fished under trees and overhanging bankside vegetation. Look for shaded food lanes with rising fish.

Hook: Standard dry-fly hook size 16 and 18.

Body: Peacock herl.

Back: Black foam pulled over the body tightly and tied down. Clip so there is a small head poking forward over the eye of the hook. Try orange foam without the extra head for ladybirds or, on a size 14 hook, the soldier beetle.

Look for shaded 'food lanes' with rising fish when there is no sign of olives or other flies, and fish it dead-drift.

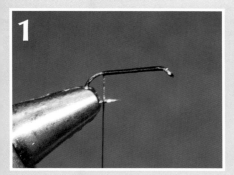

Take the thread to the bend.

Tie in a slip of 1.5 mm foam about 2 mm wide which has been tapered at the tie in point.

Catch in 2/3 peacock herls.

Twist herls round thread anticlockwise and form the body almost to the eye.

Pull the foam forward and tie off behind the eye. Trim close and whip finish.

In larger sizes the foam can be trimmed to leave a head section pointing out over the eye. A small hackle can also be added.

TERRESTRIALS – Fly box suggestions for those purchasing their flies.

Below are just a few from many patterns available from good tackle shops and fly-tyers.

Black Gnat – size 16 to 20.
Hawthorn – size 12 and 14.
Daddy Long Legs – size 10 and 12.
Foam Black Beetle – size 16 and 18.
Ant patterns – size 14 to 16. Try to get red and black versions.

Fish, Frogs, Crayfish and Small Mammals

Trout, especially large ones, are carnivorous by nature and feed hard on large food items when they can. Some become quite cannibalistic and think nothing of devouring their own kind given the chance.

SMALL FISH

Any species of small fish are fair game and perch, roach, rudd, minnows, bullheads, lampreys and even smaller trout all fall victim. Indeed, as a young teenager learning to fish, I first fished for and caught trout using either worms or lip-hooked live minnows on the Dorset Stour. I have also witnessed the wholesale slaughter of young roach shoals at Chew Valley Lake by groups of trout, clearly working together. They herded the shoals of fry into the shallows before driving them against the bank, where there was no escape, then charging into the packed shoals, using their bulk to stun the small fry before coming back to mop up the injured bait fish. I would not be without a decent fry pattern or two on any water, including trout streams if their use is permitted. On lakes where there is serious fry-feeding activity it will pay to have a floating fry pattern as well as the normal streamer style although I have greased up a streamer and fished it in the film with some

Brook lamprey moving stones prior to spawning

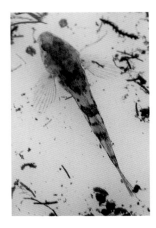

Bullhead or miller's thumb

success when fish are feeding on the surface. The classic sign of fry-feeding activity is small fish bursting out and skittering about on the surface but often all you will see is the odd dead or injured fry drifting on the surface where the fish are attacking the shoals deep down among the weeds.

FROGS

These are also fair game at times and I have handled fish with frog's legs still visible in their throats on a number of occasions. There are numerous deer-hair or popper frog patterns to be seen at fly-tying shows and in the more specialist fly shops but, as I do not have my own pattern for these I am not describing dressings for them. Fish will sometimes feed avidly on the tadpoles when they are available.

Tadpole. Note its rear legs showing. Also note the ramshorn snail – another popular trout food

VOLES AND OTHER SMALL RODENTS

An important food source, especially in some of the arctic tundra regions of the world. I have even seen trout on the Derbyshire Wye trying to dislodge voles working close to the water and, when in New Zealand a few years back, I was told that the season after I was there was going be a particularly good one for large trout. This was because there had been a glut of Manuka berries which meant there would be large numbers of a particular mouse that feeds on these berries and the trout liked to feed on these mice. Tying mouse patterns using trimmed deer-hair has become a high art form at fly-tying shows these days and there is no doubt that they work well in the right circumstances.

*Common frog
– popular food
with larger fish*

THE CRAYFISH

Where present the crayfish is well liked, especially by larger fish, and offers a very substantial meal. Large is, of course, a relative term as I have found remains of 3" long crayfish in wild fish of less than 2lbs taken on the River Lathkill when it had its own population of native crayfish. This was before the onset of 'the plague' which all but wiped out the indigenous crayfish. Here a 2lb wild trout was classed as a large fish. I do not use a crayfish imitation but there are patterns available if you search hard, with one by Dave Whitlock coming to mind.

ROACH FRY

Based on a Chew Valley favourite from the 1970s I use it when after fry feeders in large lakes where there are roach shoals.

Hook: Size 2 to 6 long shank hook or silver Aberdeen salt water hook.

Thread: White UTC 140 or similar.

Body: Pearl Krystal Chenille or similar. Other options are UTC opal tinsel over a tapered thread base or white baby wool ribbed silver tinsel, which is the original pattern I used.

Hackle: Hot orange, doubled and wound.

Wing: Layered – white goat under two or three strands of pearl or light blue Krystal Flash under light blue goat under light blue Krystal Flash under black goat to create a mobile wing. Use a ratio of 3:2:1 with the colours as you don't want too much colour. Arctic fox or Arctic runner for the smaller patterns and Icelandic sheep for the larger patterns are also excellent.

Head: White tying thread built up. Add small stick-on red eyes or painted eyes in smaller sizes. Mark the top of the head with a black or dark olive marker and epoxy over.

By substituting mixed yellow under olive goat for the blue under black goat, using gold coloured eyes and making a couple of dark smudges on the flanks with a marker pen you have a Perch Fry, or, by substituting golden olive for the blue and using a red hackle you have a Rudd Fry.

This fly is fished dead drift to sink and then lifted smoothly to the top like an ascending nymph, before re-casting. Quite a lot of takes come on the drop or before the lift presumably because of the mobile nature of the tail. N.B.. Check your fishery rules as not all river fisheries will allow this one.

Take thread down hook and tie in body material and rib if there is one. Take thread forward to about 10/15 turns of the eye.

Form the body and rib it if necessary.

Double the hackle and tie in by tip. Wind two turns and pull fibres down as you tie off.

Tie in a bunch if white arctic fox or similar then tie in a couple of strands of Krystal Flash by their centre's and double them.

Repeat this for both the blue section and then black section of the wing. Each section is just shorter than the one before it.

Build a large neat head and add some stick on eyes. Epoxy to finish. Darken the top of the head if you wish.

FISH, FROGS, CRAYFISH AND VOLES – **Fly box suggestions for those purchasing their flies.**

Below are just a few from many patterns available from good tackle shops and fly-tyers.

Hook Sizes 2 to 10
Roach Fry
Appetiser
Missionary – the version with a flat wing so that it flutters when fished on the drop.
Perch Fry – various options available.
Sculpin – especially for rivers.
Black and Silver Leech – for rivers, especially where there are brook lampreys.
Black-nosed Dace – where there are minnows present.

A Last Cast

In the Introduction to this book I said I would explain how to read the water, how the trout in particular behaves, and what it feeds on. I hope I have achieved that in a simple, easy-to-understand way and encouraged you to look closely at the water and its surroundings before you start. Just take a minute or two to look at the water you are going to fish. Look carefully at the cobwebs, search under the leaves on the bushes, study the varying currents or, on a lake, check, for wind effects, rocky outcrops, deeps and shallows before you rush off with the rod. It will pay huge dividends in the long term.

As a very young man I worked in a surveyor's office and one of my mentors was ex-army. One day, while we were doing some field work, he had given me the lead as a training exercise. When we had finished he pointed out that I had missed something. This meant we had to go back over some of the ground to make sure we had got things right. When we talked about it afterwards he gave me a bit of advice about rushing into things. I remember it well after all these years. What he said was "Time spent in reconaissance is seldom if ever wasted," something he had been taught at basic infantry training. I have never forgotten that advice and try to be true to it every time I go out. I recommend that advice to you.

Remember, every water you fish is different and so needs to be looked at independently to find the fish feeding areas. In a river every surface blemish or current change indicates the presence of something beneath the surface, whether it be a rock, weedbed or other obstruction. On a lake ripples created by a light breeze, or waves with foam lines on a windier day, can indicate possible fish feeding zones. Islands and even belts of trees can funnel the wind, creating 'food lanes' downwind, whilst colour changes in the water can signify deeps, shallows, weed beds and drop-offs; all potential fish holding spots. Every water you fish has features that govern where the fish are likely to be at any given time in the day. It is your job to learn what to look for and I hope this book will help you.

Each time you fish the hatches of fly and other available food must be identified in order to get the most out of your day. This does not have to be at a scientific level but just enough to establish fly type i.e. upwing, caddis and so on, together with size and colour variations. Continued vigilance during the day should show how the various hatches are progressing and when other flies come into the reckoning. It will also show you when certain egg-laying flies are migrating upriver to a suitable point to complete the egg-laying process. Simply watching the upwinged flies in flight will tell you which ones are hatching, when mating is going to take place, and which flies are coming back to lay their eggs. If fishing sub-surface then focus on depth as fish will alter their feeding depth according to various factors which include light, oxygen levels and the hatch stage or behaviour of their food choice of the moment. It may be necessary to fish at several different depths during the course of one fishing day.

The artificial flies I have given are some of the ones I use and are all successful patterns. This does not mean I am not looking to improve on them, or working on yet more patterns, for I am always doing that. However, they do work and cover most of the stages you will find during a hatch or fall of fly. All you have to do is recognise what is going on and 'Match the Hatch,' whether you choose to use my patterns or others of your own choice. Even better, develop patterns of your own design. This, for me at least, is the very pinnacle of success. N.B. The dressing tips for my flies have assumed some knowledge of fly dressing but even a beginner should be able to cope with a little guidance.

CASTING

Whilst it was never the purpose of this book to go into fly casting I must stress the importance of being able to cast well. This does not mean casting a long line, although at certain times this is a useful attribute. What I am saying is that you need to be able to cast accurately, and even more importantly, delicately. Presentation is the name of the game in flyfishing and the man who can place his fly delicately over a feeding fish is going to be more successful than the clumsy caster. Taking into consideration what I have said about keeping the line low over the water where possible, it pays to be able to side cast off either shoulder, especially on rivers, although it is also very useful in a boat when stalking fish, as, for example, during a caenis hatch. The cost of a casting lesson is well worth the money for both the beginner and experienced angler. Learn to cast delicately as well as to cast into a wind, especially on a river where you cannot always use the breeze to your advantage. If you happen to be going fishing for bonefish on the salt flats then fast accurate casting in a wind is a must. Get a casting lesson!

I have quoted Izaak Walton with 'study to be quiet' earlier in the book, but I would extend this to include 'study to be unseen' as well, at least as much as possible. The most successful anglers I know keep low and wear clothes that suit their fishing environment. They move slowly and quietly and often sit for long periods watching the water and the fish's behaviour without casting at all. They weigh up the chances of line shadow or flash from their casting position and what type of cast is needed, be it a roll cast, side cast or overhead cast. Only when they are satisfied with their approach and fly selection will they actually attempt to cover the fish.

PRESENTATION

This is a word I have used a lot as a flyfishing guide/instructor and I place great emphasis on it. In fact, I have been known to say that the three most important things when fly fishing are "Presentation, presentation and presentation." The word presentation encapsulates all the elements that go into actually casting the fly to the fish. These elements include choosing the correct cast so that the line travelling through the air does not spook the fish with flash or shadow, dropping the fly on the water delicately and on course so that it travels into the fish's feeding zone without drag, whether it be a dry fly, nymph or wet fly. On lakes this means setting your drift or anchoring correctly so that you can cover the fish properly without spooking it. In order to be able to make a good presentation of an imitative fly to a feeding fish it is necessary to have been observant, to have read the water correctly, to have identified the fly, or hatch stage of the fly, and to have planned your approach and the type of cast you will need. Indeed, this is why the main title of the book is *Observation*. Without good observation, chances are you will not be able to get into position to practice your presentation no matter how good your casting is.

Do I always get it right? The honest answer is "No". When I get it wrong I try to work out where I went wrong and learn from it. When I get it right I try to file the good information for future use and to pass on to others. Upon reflection perhaps the honest answer to the question "Do I always get it right" should really be "I wish!!".

I hope you find some little snippet of information in this book that will help you to more fishing success.

Tight lines